Time's Shadow

Time's

Shadow

Remembering a Family Farm in Kansas

ARNOLD J. BAUER

University Press of Kansas

Published by the University Press of Kansas (Lawrence, Kansas 66045), which was organized by the Kansas Board of Regents and is operated and funded by Emporia State University, Fort Hays State University, Kansas State University, Pittsburg State University, the University of Kansas, and Wichita State University

Library of Congress Cataloging-in-Publication Data

Bauer, Arnold J.
Time's shadow : remembering a family farm in Kansas / Arnold J. Bauer.
p. cm.
Includes bibliographical references.
ISBN 978-0-7006-1843-9 (cloth : alk. paper)
1. Bauer, Arnold J. 2. Bauer, Arnold J.—Family. 3. Farm life—Kansas—Clay County. 4. Frontier and pioneer life—Kansas—Clay County. 5. Family farms—Kansas—Clay County. 6. Clay County (Kan.)—History. 7. Clay County (Kan.)—Biography.
I. Title.
F687.C55B38 2012
978.1'275—dc23   2012005824

Printed in the United States of America

10 9 8 7 6 5 4 3 2 1

For

LILY

FRANK

&

GEORGE

The end of all our exploring
Will be to arrive where we started
And know the place for the first time.

T. S. Eliot, *Little Gidding*

Time flies over us, but leaves its shadow behind.

Nathaniel Hawthorne, *The Marble Faun*

Contents

List of Illustrations

Preface

The 160-acre family farm and the one-room rural school were the bedrock institutions of eastern Kansas from first settlement, in the 1860s, to their demise a century later, in the 1960s. The men, women, and children who created this rural world were part of the broad migratory flow that populated the United States and spilled over into Kansas. Mainly from Europe, most immigrants to Kansas came through New York; some went up the Hudson River, across the Erie Canal, and over the Great Lakes to settle first in Indiana and Illinois before pushing farther west. Still others entered through New Orleans, clawing their way up the Mississippi and Missouri rivers, beating against the current.

The new European immigrants loaded their meager belongings onto wagons (covered or not); guarded carefully their few horses, mules, livestock, and rudimentary equipment; endured the bitter cold; and bore up under the garish sun, stiff winds, and the frequent droughts that withered their first crops. They declared their intention to become citizens, staked out their homesteads, planted trees, dug wells, built coarse sod or wooden houses, and soon cobbled together the first one-room schools to educate their children in this harsh but promising land. Within a few years, wagons and rail carried their grain and livestock to the markets of Chicago, St. Louis, and beyond.

For these homesteaders and their descendants, this was the beginning of a way of life turning around family and farm, school, community, and church. These family farmers rode out the ups and downs of the nineteenth century, survived the Great Depression of the 1930s, and prospered during World War II. Then, for reasons hard at first for them to comprehend, their farms could no longer yield an income commensurate with their own and their children's ever rising expectations. By the 1960s, more and more of the smaller farms—of

80, 160, 240 acres—were sold off, the original homesteads absorbed into much larger and more productive units created by improved seeds, powerful farm machinery, global markets, and a new class of more efficient farmer-entrepreneurs. The original houses and farm buildings were bulldozed into piles of stone and shattered boards; creeks were straightened and trees uprooted. After the century-long creation of a distinct and often rewarding rural culture, our family farmers turned out the lights. They and their offspring sought jobs in Clay Center, Wichita, or Topeka; others moved to California. The hundred-year cycle ended with neither a bang nor a whimper but with the moving on of the young and the silent dying-off of the old.

———◆◆———

How can we recover the memory of that experience? How can we record not only the bare facts of existence but also *know* and *feel* something of the trials and joys, the pain and accomplishment? How can we gain a sense of a way of life in a world now gone? One path is through letters, diaries and old photo albums, common stories—including grandma's and grandpa's tales—and other eyewitness testimony. The leisure time required to write letters or keep diaries in these early years of settlement, however, was usually the privilege of middle-class city folk; common farm people usually had more pressing tasks. And there's a problem with personal testimony: the eyewitnesses are dying off. This creates a certain urgency since those who lived through the Great Depression of the 1930s or World War II are, like the author, pushing eighty; if we don't put down our stories, there'll be no one left to do so.

But then, the question is, why should anyone read stories about long-past Kansas farms and the people who lived on them? The people depicted in this book were usually not notable, nor particularly heroic or virtuous; they didn't always persevere and win out. They had their debts and doubts; they could be mean and small-minded. But at the same time there is, I believe, something fundamental that we can learn from their experience. Their struggle and the very harshness of the landscape itself impelled a commitment to family, community cooperation, and fair play. The new settlers' farms were *family* farms: husbands, wives, and children formed not only an affective unit but also an economic axis. All members had to identify with, and commit themselves to, the enterprise. If no wife, then no hearth or home—and no sales of butter and eggs to supplement the family income. If no children, then no (unpaid) farmhands. All of my family members talked not about our father's or mother's job, but about *our* farm, *our* wheat, and *our* calves. The same principles of moral economy applied to the community: if rain threatened the hay, neighbors pitched in to help save it. Exchanges were sealed with a handshake; the common agreement: "whatever is right."

Stories that provide a close-up view of another culture are not only—at best—entertaining; they also give a sense of why people thought about things the way they did. We are then led to wonder why *we* think about things the way *we* do. Pondering that question enriches our understanding of our own present lives. I hope that this account of farms and people in Goshen Township, Clay County, Kansas, framed within a century-long narrative of struggle, survival, and demise, will resonate not only with older compatriots whose experience is similar to mine, but above all, with students, young and old, and with those fellow Kansans whose curiosity leads them to wonder about a world we have lost.

Acknowledgments

I am pleased to acknowledge the many conversations with cousins and friends in Kansas regarding our common background and experience in the 1930s, 40s, and 50s, and most particularly, reminiscences with Ralph and Alfred Lang, Harold Riechers, Kyle Bauer, Gene Bauer, Erma Alexander, and Ronnie and Walter Knitter, Jr., and no doubt others whose names have slipped through my cranial sieve.

To my patient, long-suffering friends, critics, and colleagues in California and elsewhere—a list too long to display here—I apologize for inflicting upon them my enthusiasms, long harangues, and early versions of this project over dinners and afternoon coffees. I am indebted and feel grateful to all for their forgiving and helpful responses. There are three people, however, to whom I owe special thanks: Danielle Greenwood, as always, was relentlessly encouraging; Jo Burr Margadant's keen-eyed common sense more than once saved me from myself; and Kathy Polkinghorn gave me the benefit of her literary suggestions.

Further afield, in Chile, my forty-five-year-long friendship with Carlos Hurtado Ruíz-Tagle ignited my interests in other rural worlds and gave me perspective on my own.

My beloved daughter, Rebecca Bauer, and her family accompanied me on two recent visits to my native land, for which I am enormously grateful. She, too, though resident in New York City, has Kansas in her heart.

Kathy Haney, curator of the Clay Center Museum, and James Beck, director of the Wakefield Museum, were generous with their time and knowledge of Clay County.

Finally, my profound thanks to Fred Woodward, director of the University Press of Kansas, for his tireless support and for—once only—changing his mind. Sara Henderson White, Larisa Martin, Susan Schott, Martha Whitt, and other cheerful professionals at UPK have been a pleasure to work with.

Time's Shadow

1
The Beginning

During the past several million years, powerful glaciers covered a large swath of North America, grinding their way back and forth at a snail's pace in their relentless advance and retreat. Hundreds of thousands of years slowly passed until the last ice age reached its southernmost penetration some 600,000 years ago, sculpting what is now the northeastern corner of Kansas, and in its wake leaving behind the flora and fauna, the soils, rivers, and creeks that eventually would make up the terrain of what became communities of 160-acre family farms.

The last glacier created in this part of Kansas a landscape of low rolling hills that are visible today from the ruined front porch of my own former family home, while leaving underfoot a varied debris of sediments of clay, sand, and gravel; and—most important, for the immigrant farmers to come—a fine, rich, windborne silt known as *loess*, or "loose" soil, the basis for virtual oceans of grassland (called "prairies" by seventeenth-century French Jesuit missionaries), and the rich loam of creek and river valleys. In their powerful advance the glaciers rearranged what would become the Missouri, Kansas, and Big Blue rivers; upon retreat, the melting ice left the new rivers and streams swollen with slow, turbid water.[1]

Much more recently, only some 35,000 years ago, the first people slowly entered this landscape. Far away to the northwest of our continent, a human family led other emigrants to cross over Beringia, the ice bridge that then linked Asia with America, opening a door onto a new land. These early hunters and gatherers moved down the Pacific littoral, some afoot, others by boat, striking inland when climate, geography, and resources permitted, leaving behind the dead carcasses of native mammals, which, assisted by changes in climate and vegetation, they hunted to extinction. Finally, after an exceedingly long and slow trek, they reached the far southern extreme of the Western hemisphere about 14,000 years ago, leaving traces of their culture at the present archeological site of Monte Verde in Chilean Patagonia.[2]

In the course of their long advance, the descendants of the Bering immigrants spread unevenly over most of the vast continents of North and South America. They were slow to penetrate the formidable western mountain ranges and intimidating deserts but eventually managed to explore the North American plains, reaching the grasslands of what is now Kansas as early as 11,000 years ago.

The newcomers' numbers increased as they came to terms with a new geography. They survived the rolling advance of prairie fire and smoke ignited by careless cooks and lightning and were not yet exposed to the deadly pathogens carried by later invaders. They foraged for sustenance among unfamiliar plants and fruit, hunted for deer and beaver, found streams foaming with fish. Searching for meat and thick hides for protection against the cold, they undertook the difficult task—on foot, with flint-tipped arrows and spears—of killing the woolly bison that were themselves, in ages past, also immigrants from Asia.

Thousands of years later, in the sixteenth century, the offspring of these original immigrants encountered Spaniards pushing into northern Mexico; and then, three centuries after that, they met head-on the mainly Anglo-Germanic Protestants advancing into Kansas from the east. The long-established residents, misnamed "Indians," must surely have thought of themselves as "natives" to the land. The Great Plains, after all, had been their abode for many centuries, indeed, millennia. They had become intimately familiar with the lay of the land; knew the great rivers, mountains, plains, and flora and fauna of their ancestral homelands; were impressive trappers, hunters, and rudimentary agriculturists. They brought to high development the breeding and training of the horses they acquired from the Spanish invaders who followed in the track of Vásquez de Coronado. They left their mark not just in the innumerable place-names, but also in the history they later shared with the newcomers pressing westward from the new United States.

When the European immigrants poling upstream on the Missouri River from St. Louis arrived in eastern Kansas, they shared at first an edgy coexistence with the original inhabitants. Faced with the seemingly relentless tide of history, the natives were prepared to negotiate their fate; and when that failed, to fight to the end to preserve their way of life. Subsequent conflict in the course of the nineteenth century against better-armed and increasingly numerous immigrants of European origin, along with imported epidemic disease, doomed the original nations to defeat and near-extinction.

Having been brought up as a kid reading Cyrus Townsend Brady's multivolume *Indian Fights and Fighters* (1904), a celebration of the "winning of the West," it was some time before I came to understand that Kansas history did not begin with the names of German immigrants that I saw on the tombstones in the Schaubel Cemetery.

One unrecorded day in the summer of 1868, my maternal great-grandfather, Ferdinand Alexander, and his wife, Friedrieke, after having located the proper markings made by the General Surveyor's Office, staked out on the Kansas frontier in Goshen Township, Clay County, a section of virgin land by placing limestone markers at the four corners of what was to be their 160-acre homestead. Many of the elements in the long-term process we've just traced were present and helped shape the nature of their farm. All around were the rolling hills, the tall stretches of ungrazed prairie grass nurtured by the loess-rich soil. Just a hundred yards north of the homestead, a still undefiled creek wound its way eastward over the watershed to the Big Blue and on to the Kansas River, both carved by the last glacier.

Even the original inhabitants were close at hand: when Ferdinand Alexander rode west that summer to file his claim at the Concordia Land Office—Clay Center's was not yet open for business—the memory of battle cries and rifle fire would have been fresh in people's minds. The Cheyenne, descendants of the people who had crossed over Beringia thousands of years before, were engaged in fierce conflict with Custer's Seventh Cavalry based at Fort Hays on the Smoky Hill River. My great-grandfather Alexander could not have imagined the silent millennia of time past, or the thousands of humans that preceded his arrival, or that his daring enterprise of founding a family farm on the Kansas frontier represented only a tiny sliver on the long spectrum of geologic time.

2
Family

My ancestors were part of the 7 million German immigrants who came to the United States in successive waves beginning in the late seventeenth century. The early arrivals were mainly Mennonites in quest of religious freedom. A second, fairly small group came to the United States after their liberal project for a unified Germany failed in the revolution of 1848. Many of these idealistic immigrants fought on the Union side during the American Civil War. Apparently my great-grandfather Ferdinand Alexander, born in 1817, and great-grandmother Friedrieke, born four years earlier, migrated out of this background. They were educated people. Their three sons—Ronald, Arnold, and Robert—all had studied for the Lutheran clergy, while Ferdinand, once in the United—or rather, the Disunited—States, became an officer in the Indiana infantry during the Civil War. Taking advantage of privileges awarded to army veterans, Ferdinand moved west and three years after the war, established his homestead, forming the "Alexander home place" in Goshen Township. I have no knowledge of his first house. Did he, like the Lang family who homesteaded the adjacent farm, burrow into a sod dugout? Were his "prairie schooner children"

> "Born beneath the stars,
> Beneath falling snow,
> With no physician there,
> Except a Kansas prayer,
> With the Indian raid a howling through the air?"[1]

Ferdinand Alexander's son Robert Jakob (my grandfather, born in 1853) and his wife, Mary Rebecca (b. 1862), produced eight children, including my mother, Anna Elizabeth Alexander. She married my father, Francis William Bauer, in 1921. Their children were two daughters, Lucille Marie and Irene Mary, and a son, the writer of these stories.

Robert Jakob Alexander died young at forty-three in 1896, some say in a woman's arms, not those of his wife. The widow, Mary Rebecca, left alone at thirty-five with eight children—from Reinhold, the eldest at fifteen, down to my mother, a baby of six months—marshaled the forces of her young family to wrest a living and then a surplus out of the hard soil of a quarter section of Kansas upland. I later wondered not only how but also why Mary Rebecca Alexander had done this. Many farmers with strong sons and better land had gone under, wrenched into bankruptcy by bad weather and the brutal cycles of world prices. Did she feel compelled to finish what her husband had started? Had she forced herself to mobilize a clutch of children in order to assuage the loss of a beloved mate? Or was it just what one did, given the circumstances? In any case, it was a widely remarked feat, still remembered while I was growing up.

Grandma Alexander died at eighty in 1942. I remember her as thin and bent, almost always in a pale print dress, sitting silent on the concrete front porch of her family's homestead, looking—as anyone but a kid would have understood—utterly worn-out after a hard life. But, I, of course, unaware of her long struggle, thought she was just old.

A third and much larger wave of German immigrants came to the United States and Kansas in the 1870s and 80s. In contrast to the earlier German immigrants, many of these newcomers were more humble folk seeking free or cheap land beyond the Missouri. Johann Jakob Bauer (1838–1917), my paternal great-grandfather, was one of twelve family members living on a small peasant holding near the village of Steinheim an der Murr, Württemberg, Swabia. The final notation (1882) in the civil registry of that town regarding my great-grandfather reads, "*nach Amerika gegangen*"—gone to America. Another, and compelling, motive for migration in this era was the fear of conscription into the German Army at a time of accelerated European militarization.

Johann Jakob and Katharina Albrecht (1841–1924) were somehow able to acquire what became the 320-acre "Bauer home place" in the 1880s.[2] That farm passed to my grandfather Wilhelm Jakob Bauer and his wife, the dour Nettie. They, in turn, managed to acquire four additional 160-acre farms, one of which was assigned to my father and where I was born in 1931, at home, fifteen unpaved miles from the nearest doctor, with my aunt Helen serving as midwife. My older sisters, Irene and Lucille, grew up and after high school fled the farm as quickly as propriety permitted.

I might add, in order to reveal the literally anonymous beginning of my life, that even my name was accidental. Immediately after my birth, and most probably preceding it, an irresolvable dispute arose over what I should be called. My mother wanted Robert, my father insisted on William; one sister wanted Leroy—of all things—the other sister something else. Finally after several *weeks* of stalemate, four names were scrawled on scraps of paper, placed in a hat, and "Arnold," a name I've never liked, was drawn out. However, a clerk in the Clay Center Courthouse, apparently bored with my family's dithering—but without informing them of his action—sent in his *own* preference, the improbable "Walter Lloyd," to the state capital. I discovered this bizarre occurrence nineteen years later when the U.S. Air Force demanded a birth certificate for enlistment. I drove to Topeka, found my parents' own birth certificates in the records, and was able to persuade a clerk that, in fact, I did exist.

3
A Farm in Kansas

We had a farm in Kansas, 160 acres exactly 10 miles north and 5 east of the county seat of Clay Center. Unlike the relentless plain farther west where a thin snow blows horizontally across the short wheat stubble and tumbleweeds cartwheel in the arid wind out beyond the 100th Meridian, this part of northeast Kansas is a land of gently rolling hills and tree-lined creeks. Not quite as idyllic as Dorothy's Land of Oz; nevertheless, some 35 inches of annual rainfall create an often-verdant landscape drained by the abundant Blue, Smoky Hill, Republican, and Kansas rivers that flow into the broad Missouri at Kansas City. The quality of soil varies from farm to farm and even field to field, with tough gumbo side by side with rich black bottom-land. It is also a harsh land of unpredictable drought, violent yellowish purple thunderstorms that blow up out of the southwest, and, not uncommonly, cyclones that touch the ground, twisting their way along in a funnel of dust, flying boards, and tree limbs, tracking to the northeast and sometimes exploding the walls of houses while leaving, oddly enough, the stove, table, and chairs in place. The winter temperature dips down to 10 to 12 degrees below zero, producing ice and fierce blizzards so dense that a rope line is occasionally needed to find one's way from the house to feed the cattle. People tell of the boy who put his damp tongue on a frozen axe blade with dire consequences (but no one I know has actually seen such an event). In any case, it was no country for the fainthearted.

In 1854, seven years before Kansas became a state and nearly a decade before the first Homestead Act became law on January 1, 1863, the

U.S. General Surveyor's Office, anticipating the future conquest of the country, projected an imaginary grid marked by small bronze markers and foot-square limestone pillars across an entire territory long occupied by a number of different Native American tribes. Fixing an "Initial Point" at the intersection of the 40th Parallel (the Kansas-Nebraska border) and the Sixth Principal Meridian, the surveyors staked off *counties* and *townships*, which in turn were divided, as a rule, into 36 square miles. Each square mile was then subdivided into four *sections* of 160 acres each, an area thought to be appropriate for the family-farmer homesteaders to come.

The formal settlement of this part of Kansas took place as a result of the first and subsequent Homestead Acts, which were designed primarily to grant land to heads of household, usually married men over twenty-one, or Union Army veterans, in order to foster permanent settlement. Homesteaders were required to pay a registration fee, improve the property, and live on it—sleep on it!—for five years. Widows, and single women over twenty-one, if heads of household, were also eligible. Married women were *not* eligible so as to prevent a double grant to a conjugal union. On the other hand, a single woman could acquire a homestead grant and then marry a single man who had previously acquired a grant. In our neighborhood, we see such an occurrence in the case of Jacobina Lang, the matriarch of our long-term neighbors the Lang family, who established her homestead in 1870. Jacobina soon married and lived with her new husband in a sod house, partly dug out of a hillside that is still visible on a meadow near our farm. She must also have brought from Germany to decorate her future prairie home the seeds to establish the phlox flowers that according to her great-grandson, Ralph Lang, voluntarily reappear every spring but *only* near the old dugout.

Jacobina and her husband buried two of their children, who died shortly after birth, near the dugout and later removed their bodies to the cemetery—later called the Schaubel Cemetery—that she established on an acre of her homestead. Just to the north and west of our pioneer families, the people Willa Cather wrote about in her unforgettable *My Ántonia* struggled to form their own settlements in the new state of Nebraska—all part of the rolling tide of immigrants, who were devoted to the land and brutal to its original inhabitants and their buffalo.

Within two decades following the first Homestead Act, the eastern third of Kansas was occupied under those provisions. By 1880, nearly 80,000 immigrants, mainly from Europe, had acquired over 10.5 million acres in Kansas—more than one-fifth of Kansas and nearly twice the total area of Massachusetts—divided mostly into 160-acre lots.[1] Until very recently, this had been a frontier world. Enormous herds of bison, many deer, beaver, and coyotes—all kinds of wild animals and birds—still lived on these riverbanks and lush grasslands along with thousands of Kiowa, Osage, Kansas, Cheyenne, Ponca, and other Native Americans.

At about this time, in 1871, James Butler "Wild Bill" Hickok was the marshal of Abilene, Kansas, a cow town just 40 miles to the south of the Alexander homestead. Close by, another "Bill"—William Cody, later known as the showman "Buffalo Bill"—grew up riding his pony bareback, hunting buffalo, and guiding wagon trains westward. The deep-grooved wagon tracks, overgrown by the prairie grass, are still visible, running through the country where my great-grandparents homesteaded and made great efforts to survive.

In those same years, the bloody battles between pro- and anti-slavery factions to determine the nature of statehood (Kansas was admitted to the Union in 1861) were a very recent memory. Nor could Great-Grandfather Ferdinand Alexander have been unaware of another common occurrence of those times: George Grey, an early settler, reported that the year before Ferdinand homesteaded, a herd of thousands of Texas longhorns had passed through the eastern part of Clay County on their way from Abilene to Leavenworth, leaving tracks that remained in the land for several years.

I've often wondered what these first families felt crossing into Kansas and moving west, looking ahead over the rolling prairie to the endless horizon, trying to anticipate the unseen perils. I imagine them exhausted from the interminable search for food and water, the anxiety over their children and babies, and the sleepless days on the jolting, lurching wagon. I see the men wet but unwashed, heavy-footed in clumsy shoes, slogging alongside their oxen or broad-backed horses, braced against the wind and slanting rain of a Kansas thunderstorm, wagering everything on this plunge into the unknown. Would not their thoughts inevitably have turned back to the scant, 12-acre peasant plot they'd left behind in Germany? Did doubt not creep into their thoughts about whether an almost unimaginable landmass of 160 acres would actually, really, be theirs for the payment of a tiny fistful of dollars?

The early homesteaders are easily, but improperly, romanticized. The actual legislation governing the distribution of land was a bureaucratic nightmare filled with complicated restrictions and procedures that were constantly amended. Then, once the pioneer settler was actually able to determine the boundaries of an unclaimed 160 acres, he or she would have driven the team of oxen or horses to Junction City or Concordia—the nearest land offices—to file the claim and pay the fees. Then, the new homesteader would have returned to the vacant lot, helped the children to step down, unloaded the wagon, and scanned the nearly limitless horizon. After all of this, the need for the most rudimentary elements of basic existence, food and shelter, must have seemed overwhelming. The pioneers had to break the heavy virgin sod, plant trees and crops, build fences, either burrow into the sides of low hills or find the poles and branches for simple houses. Small wonder that more than 60 percent of early homesteaders in eastern Kansas failed to make a go of it.

In any case, there they were, our ancestors. With little knowledge to go on, they tried to come to grips with an alien landscape, wondering which elements of the world they knew might be appropriate to the new land and which should be discarded. They eyed the low-lying swales for traces of scarce and indispensable water and then dug by hand deep wells walled with rocks. Ours was over 30 feet deep with several harmless bull snakes living among the cool rock walls.

Unaccustomed to the new terrain, settlers tried to figure out which soils—upland or bottomland—would best produce crops. In the years of first settlement, they occasionally—but mistakenly—plowed the thin-soil slopes held together by native prairie grass, thinking the bottomlands too heavy and wet. Soon they discovered that the alluvial lowlands held the best soils. Dependent on domestic animals, they transplanted the entire menagerie of European cows, pigs, and chickens, treasuring especially their scarce cattle and horses almost as if they were their true children. Our immigrant families were not the heroic cavalry of Western lore, but rather the foot soldiers—*pionniers* in the original meaning of the French word—of settlement driven on by hope for cheap land and freedom from military conscription in their European homelands. While their aims were often fulfilled, their dreams in these early years must have been filled with despair and longing for the overcrowded but relatively secure Swabian villages they had left behind.

Once settled on a quarter section, the homesteaders huddled silently in storm cellars during the sudden and violent thunderstorms, were assailed by the hail and tornadoes that sweep through this country, endured the bitter cold, bore up under the boiling summer sun and frequent droughts that withered the crops. And then, relieved and pleased when the cuttings of apple trees and vines budded forth, the potatoes sprouted, the cattle calved, they could imagine that there was a future after all. This was the beginning of a brief, century-long cycle, a way of life, an impressive accomplishment.

My great-grandparents and their fellow homesteaders created out of this land of prairie grass and black river bottomland a farming community they thought would be as long-lasting as the peasant villages they'd left behind. They built stone and sturdy wooden houses, planting trees for generations to come. In fact, their new world dream lasted a scant century, from the 1860s when our people homesteaded in Goshen Township to the 1960s when circumstances they didn't anticipate and barely understood swept them into the dustbin of history.

Our farm was never an idyll—a place that city people sometimes romanticize and more often disdain—but rather a quarter section of a square mile won through relentless work against cold, drought, clouds of grasshoppers, and fierce storms. A third of the farm, the upland hilly part, remained in native prairie grass never broken by

The author as a young man.

the plow. The rest of the land our ancestors cultivated and planted to wheat or oats or alfalfa, and sometimes to sorghum and sunflowers. In one memorable case, my father, in one of his many experimental modes, sowed flax. Our neighbors scorned this as foolish, which it turned out to be. He had one good harvest that he put in the granary waiting for the anticipated steep increase in price, which never came. We were cautioned never to jump into the storage bin full of the slick dark brown kernels that, like quicksand, suck in heavy objects, for fear of being swallowed up.

We had cattle and pigs, hundreds of chickens, two dogs called Jack and Sport, a couple of barn cats, a pony called Tony, two big working horses named Molly and Pete, and a team of mules. We bestowed names on dogs and cats and horses and mules; cows and pigs remained anonymous. Sheep and goats were regarded as a nuisance: the former ate the grass too close to the ground; goats were tough to eat. Although present in the years of first settlement, oxen were later thought quaint, their pace too slow to haul the mechanical mowers or grain binders in the new American landscape.

A slow, muddy stream called Fancy Creek, lined with cottonwood, elms, box elder, walnut, and oak, ran through the farm, and alongside the creek were narrow, level fields of black soil suitable for corn and for our best garden patch. There were catfish, muskrats, and raccoons in the creek; bunny rabbits in the snowy hedgerows; wild turkeys, jackrabbits, and coyotes in the open fields; bull and garter snakes and the odd rattler; and even, now and then, you saw deer and foxes. Baltimore orioles, robins, hawks, and lots of sparrows and swallows darted about, and in the spring great flocks of shiny metallic, squawking crows blackened the creekside trees looking for bugs and early corn.

I looked forward to the muskrat-trapping season that officially began on the first of December, when the animals' fur became prime, and lasted for two months. During those winter mornings I ran the line of traps that I'd set along the banks of two creeks: one, a quarter mile behind the house; the second, three-quarters of a mile in the other direction over fields of dormant wheat, sometimes covered with drifts of blowing snow.

Muskrats are semi-aquatic. In some places they build piles of sticks and grass somewhat reminiscent of small beaver lodges but in our creeks, they dug burrows into the earthen bank above the waterline and then created a second passage by digging a tunnel that led downward and emerged underwater. It's in this underwater runway that you set the trap, first by pressing your foot down on the spring mechanism of the six-inch steel jaws, carefully fixing the trigger, and then attaching the ring of the trap's 30-inch-long chain to a steel rod driven into the edge of the creek bed with a hammer. I positioned the trap so that the captured animal would drown rather than escape by chewing off its own leg. You have to be careful while setting and staking the trap not to slip down the creek bank into the freezing or frozen stream.

I ran these traplines once a day during the season. The best time is early light when muskrats have finished their nocturnal rambles.

Then, back to the house for breakfast before setting off, on foot or riding my pony, to Fairfield District #24, a mile and a half north. If I'd been lucky that morning—once, at least, I caught two in a single day—I'd separate the pelt from the animal in the afternoon.

Skinning the muskrat required patience and a steady hand. The old-style, one-edged safety razor blade made a perfect instrument. You began by driving nails through the webbed back feet of the muskrat so that its body hung head-down, legs spread wide, on the smoothed-off surface of a box elder tree in the yard. Next, you cut around and between the back legs, being careful not to slash the musk gland, pulling downward on the fur, while continuing to cut the whitish grey membrane between flesh and pelt. Then you stretched the pelt on a smooth redwood shingle, scraped off any remaining fat with a dull knife, placed a length of baling wire through a previously drilled hole, and hung the shingle on a rafter out of reach of any sniffing rat.

The cold and dry winter air preserved the pelts until we took them to the Nelson brothers fur traders in Clay Center. Their high-ceilinged warehouse alongside the Kansas Pacific railroad tracks reeked of the fat and flesh of coyote, skunk, and raccoon—perhaps even the odd deerskin, along with the muskrat pelts. You had to haggle with the Nelson brothers over price; even a small nick in the pelt knocked down its value. I seem to remember that I was paid, depending on size and quality, from $1.50 to $3.00 a pelt, and that I sold twenty to twenty-five each season. I have no memory whatsoever of what I might have bought with that fabulous amount.

<hr/>

If you are brought up as a kid on a proper farm, and you hunt along the streams, trap muskrats under shallow ice before the sun comes up in the winter, help put up firewood, plow and harvest, drive plodding workhorses sitting on a steel cultivator seat for long days in the sun, learn how to make little whistles out of green box elder shoots in the spring, and make slingshots from forked branches of oak and strips of inner tubes . . . if you do these things, you come to know every corner, every ditch and rise of the land: where the rabbits nest, where the cattle are likely to slip under the barbed wire in gullies. You develop an intense sense of place never to be lost, the details engraved in your brain and in the memories that later invade your dreams.

4
Houses

Our house, like most other farmhouses in this part of Kansas and, for that matter, like many throughout the Midwest, was a two-story wood frame building in the shape of a T, with a solid foundation, a stone-walled cellar, and screened-in porches on the north and south. The stem of the T was usually laid out east to west, designed to brace the cross-head of the T against cyclones that spun out of the southwest. Upstairs were four bedrooms, one shared by my sisters, another filled with tools, wires, discarded Bakelite radio parts, large crocks, and shelves of empty Mason jars. The upstairs room at the east end was reserved for the occasional hired hand, and my own feather bed was in the middle room. My parents slept downstairs in the main bedroom. When one of us became ill—say, from measles, mumps, scarlet fever, or the chicken pox—we recovered in our own rooms; but when I came down with two serious cases of pneumonia, my parents thought it necessary to present the best face for the doctor who was called out on winter roads from Clay Center. On those occasions, I was placed in the back room, officially the "parlor," and known to us for reasons unknown as the "*front* room."

Nearly all the local farmhouses had a "front room," furnished almost always with heavy, overstuffed dark bluish green chairs and a sofa; a thick walnut table with ponderous carved legs; and one or two copies of somber pastoral scenes with threatening clouds, a Protestant view, one imagines, of an Old Testament landscape. A popular decoration, present in our and in many of our neighbors' front rooms, was an inexpensive but framed copy of a painting depicting a doleful, mostly naked Indian in profile, drooping lance in hand, gazing gloomily toward *The Trail's End*.[1]

This, I suppose, represented for many—though not for the origi-

Bauer home place. This was my paternal grandparents' house and farm buildings. The main house, cistern, cellar, and smokehouse are enclosed by trees. The henhouse is on the right; the granaries, silo, and other buildings are out of sight. The corral with two-story stone and oak barn designed and built by my father is on the upper left. The pole with power transformer at the head of the driveway reveals that the picture was taken after 1939.

nal artist—the success of killing off the native population, a process not that distant from my grandparents' generation.

A front room and its furnishings came to be absolutely required by any self-respecting newly married couple setting up their own home. It was free of beds and any kind of work paraphernalia. A luxury feature was "Venetian blinds," rather than the ordinary spring-loaded, pull-down shades. My cousin Wilene, newly wed to Homer, had the first ones around and took advantage of every opportunity to mention them in company: "Why, I was just cleaning my *Venetian blinds* when. . . ." The front room, Venetian blinds or not, was off-limits to kids except for Thanksgiving and Christmas and, in our case, reserved for the rare visit from the doctor or the uninvited preacher.

The William Bauer family at the home place in the mid-1930s. Grandfather is center front, flanked by Aunt Helen and Grandmother Nettie. My father is at center back with Uncles Paul, Gerald, Alfred, and Harry alongside.

Because I associate the front room with illness and death, I should add that until Doctor Salk's vaccine became available in the early 1950s, we lived in fear of infantile paralysis (poliomyelitis) and spending the rest of our lives in an "iron lung," vividly shown in the *Look* and *Life* magazines my father subscribed to. "Polio" was thought by some to be spread by eating watermelons and by others by swimming in public pools. Since the only proper concrete swimming pool was 15 miles away in Clay Center—and because farm kids rarely if ever entered such a place (I never did)—my parents were spared that particular worry. Two kids on neighboring farms, Sonny Dankenbring and Gail Gerardy, were victims of polio, bringing the dread disease close to home.

During our waking hours indoors we lived mainly in the dining room, furnished with a round oak table with three extendable leaves (now in my house in California), oak chairs, and a large potbellied wood-burning stove for heat. The most impressive dining room piece was the polished oak buffet with curved mirror along the back, hinged doors on either side. Centered on a white doily and reflected in the mirror sat the cut glass bowl, perhaps 6 inches deep and 10 inches across, containing lesser valuables and sometimes carelessly tossed letters. While my sisters were permitted to lift the bowl to dust the buffet top, I was not allowed to touch, let alone to lift, this object that I believe was one of my parents' wedding gifts. It was pointed out more than once that it cost $25.

A year before my parents were married, in 1920, when the wedding gift of a cut glass bowl in the sophisticated worlds of New York and Princeton had already become passé, a subject of ridicule, Scott Fitzgerald published a derisively sarcastic short story, "The Cut Glass Bowl." Coming across the story recently, I recalled my mother's innocent and touching pride in what must have been—along with her diamond engagement ring—the most treasured gift she had ever received.

Also in the living room, where my father occupied a rocking chair next to the radio, *The National Geographic*, *The Saturday Evening Post*, *Popular Mechanics*, and other magazines piled up in a plywood rack. When, because of a rainwater leak, the lathe-and-plaster ceiling began to sag, F. W.—everyone called my father, Francis William, "F. W."—impetuously ripped it down one Sunday morning, showering dust and splinters all over the room, and a few days later replaced it with 4 x 4-foot squares of varnished plywood with inch-wide strips at the seams painted "Chinese red." The proudly installed Chinese red ceiling rubbed sores that took a long time to heal. For my father, the ceiling was modern and practical; for my mother, Anna Alexander, a permanent horror; and undoubtedly—although she wouldn't have had these words—an indication of fundamental differences in the way they went about things.

During the hot, sultry summer I slept on the screened-in north porch, a place that seemed to project outward into the blackness of the night. There were lots of night sounds. You knew that possums and raccoons, up from the creek, were out there skulking about silently and harmlessly. Crickets made a terrific racket, but if you listened carefully you could hear the slight movement of what most likely were horses and cattle in the barnyard. Inevitably, one's imagination came into play and the odd sounds took on a sinister meaning. Was that shuffling noise the tread of the odd bachelor who rented one of the Riechers's farms just down the road? Occasionally large, hard-backed flying bugs—known as "democrats"—crashed against the screen. But tired, I'd drop off, awakened at dawn by the relentless sun and my father's call to chores. Once (only once) at the breakfast table after a restless night, I confessed to my father my fear of the night. His solution—practical if unhelpful—was for me to imagine the farm and buildings as if the sun were up: "it's all the same out there," he pointed out, "whether it's day or night."

My father provided, or tried to provide, other examples for my personal improvement. Fearless when climbing telephone poles or windmill towers or walking on 12 x 12-inch beams on railroad trestles high over riverbeds, it was hard for him to comprehend my fear of heights. The issue became especially acute when he undertook to repair our large, fairly steep-roofed tall barn. Working my way up the more gentle slope of the shed part of the building, I was able to hand up shingles, nails, and tools to my father, but as we reached the steeper part, my courage failed and I'd press myself, leech-like, flat against the roof, immobile with fear. Discussion then followed about how silly I was being, that even if I slipped, the lower shed roof would stop the slide, there was no need to be afraid, I could see how he, much further up, was in no danger, and so on.

Finally, exasperated, he offered a bribe: if I agreed to go all the way, he'd nail a Three Musketeers candy bar for me to the top ridge. The Three Musketeers bar was my favorite and cost a nickel at the local store, but I never got to the top. When I hesitated at a second challenge, I remember—or think I remember—that he rather disdainfully abandoned the project. Whether the memory is accurate or not, the event was engraved in my brain.

Another failing was the inability to blow my nose properly. For this, as well as for roof climbing, I was compared unfavorably with

Donnie Hofmann. My father pointed out that Donnie knew how to blow *his* nose, and moreover had climbed up on another steep roof to help his father. None of this must have boosted my self-esteem at the time—and I've never got over being skittish about heights—but neither does it seem to have caused irreparable psychological damage.

⸺⸺

Until we got electricity and even for a few years afterward, Mother cooked and baked in a wood-fired, cast-iron stove and kept a few things cool in an icebox. There was a treasured cupboard in the kitchen that had deep, pull-out, curved tin flour bins and a marble counter. Here I remember her standing to knead the weekly bread, patting out trays of raisin-filled cookies for the oven, baking apple and cherry pies. Over the small oilcloth-covered breakfast table, you looked out through tall windows to flowerbeds where my mother, like most farm wives, planted seeds ordered from Henry Fields Seed and Nursery catalogues to grow hollyhocks, zinnias, canna lilies (for a long time I thought they were called "cannon" lilies), morning glories, and, I suppose, others, along with a pair of lilacs that bloomed on either side of the doorway. Further out, along the clothesline, was the indispensable vegetable garden and potato patch. A long driveway led several hundred yards to the mailbox. The entrance to the kitchen passed through a washroom that featured a cast-iron hand pump over the cistern, hooks for work clothes, a .22-caliber rifle, and a double-barreled 12-gauge shotgun; brooms, boots, and rubber overshoes stood in the corner.

Except for the cistern pump, as with every other farmhouse, we had no indoor plumbing and consequently no indoor bathroom. So we took baths standing upright in a small, galvanized tub, having heated the water in three-gallon pails on the woodstove. During the winter I believe we made do with a "good wash" with soap and washcloth. Strange to say, I cannot remember taking these baths: although infrequent, particularly during the winter, you'd think they'd be unforgettable.

Thanks to my father's restless industry, however, we did have a summertime bathing device unique to the neighborhood. A few years before the arrival of electricity and electric pumps, he somehow acquired from a railroad salvage yard a long, steel steam boiler perhaps 5 feet in diameter. He pulled it upright with ropes and pulleys onto a solid concrete base alongside the barn and piped water into it from the windmill-driven well. While you stood naked on a wooden pallet, a 4-inch horizontal spout 8 feet up the side of the standpipe opened with a pull chain to produce a powerful, overhead cascade of cold water that washed away the day's dust and fatigue.

Our farm had substantial outbuildings. There was a large barn with stanchions for eight milk cows. It will shock most city people to know that cows must be milked twice a day for much of the year—or until they go dry—rain, snow, or shine. Milking was definitely not my or my sisters' favorite chore and it was a particularly onerous task during the freezing and dark winter mornings when the cows were twitchy and loath to move into the proper position. The barn also had stalls for a team of horses and four mules, and arched above the second floor was what seemed at the time an enormous, towering hayloft.

The granary was a separate building with large bins and cribs for wheat, corn, and oats. A mechanical elevator dragged chain-linked buckets of grain up an inclined chute to the bins. This device, not very common in our neighborhood—another tribute to my father's mechanical genius—was driven by a team of mules pulling a long pole in interminable circles around a mechanism—a winch—geared to generate power to drive the conveyer. There was a long, low building for hogs, a chicken house with a straw loft, and a brooder house to incubate hundreds of young chicks. An outhouse (*without* the new moon cutout in the flat board walls) was equipped with shiny pages from old Sears & Roebuck catalogues. This completed the farmstead. The buildings, except for the hog house, were painted red with white stripes; the house, of course, was white.

5
Anna Alexander

My mother, Anna Elizabeth Alexander, was an intelligent, simple, uneducated person and knew nothing of books or music or of other places. She slept during the only movie I remember going with her to see, *The Lost Weekend*, starring Ray Milland—an exceedingly odd choice for the conventional Rex Theatre in Clay Center to present or for us to attend.

My mother was not religious and had little patience with those who she believed were hypocritical about church. She would say about religion or books or history that "it's all too much for me." She was smart, thoughtful, and had common sense and a good intuition about people. Like many of that generation, she was suspicious of the city, a term that included Clay Center, and the best thing she could say about anyone was that he or she was "just as common as an old shoe." No upward mobility striving for her.

The picture on page 25, taken when she was twenty-two, reveals a handsome, even pretty young woman and accurately suggests a character of quiet skepticism. One of eight brothers and sisters, in her early teens she worked as housekeeper in the small farm town of Leonardville some 20 miles southeast of the farm. There was plenty of work for male children on the several farms acquired by my widowed grandmother Mary Alexander in the 1920s, but it was common practice in families with sufficient male children and a surplus of single females to send the daughters out for experience and extra cash. I remember my mother as a tall, angular, warm woman who waved her arms and swore at cards and baked bread and made endless pies and cookies. She had a robust, and for the time irreverent, sense of humor. Floods of tears came to her eyes when she laughed and she was often merry.

Because later in life she was ill so long, and for the last ten years

Anna Alexander at twenty-two.

barely recognized us, it's difficult now for me to remember her full of laughter and warmth. My very earliest memory of her is the faint image—perhaps it's the memory of a dream—of a late summer evening when we came back to the house, the two of us, picking our way over the plowed fields down next to Fancy Creek, dragging along my tiny red wagon filled with new potatoes. It was already dark when we got to the house and I remember, or have a sense that I remember, the world as very large and I have no notion of what lay beyond the darkness. The two of us seemed completely alone on the planet. After that, there is a succession of memories turning around work: of her sorting eggs or bending her big frame to feed chickens, of working with her in the vegetable garden with that special scent of fresh water on tomato plants, or the satisfying look of rows of new lettuce coming through the ground. I made little dams and channels to turn the water down the rows.

I can't recall that I felt overworked. It was natural for kids to do the daily chores and, by the early teens or even earlier, for both boys and girls to begin fieldwork. I do recall my mother's occasional remark to me, hoping, I imagine, to reserve some sense of childhood joy: "Remember, you're only little once."

Once, only once that I remember—I must have been nine or ten—she gave me a sharp rap across the face. Had I been cheeky? More likely, I'd forgotten after several reminders to bring in firewood or feed the chickens: it must have been a grave offense. My father scolded me for being late in the mornings or misplacing or misusing tools, but never did he lay a hand on me. In fact, I can't remember, nor did I hear tell of anyone, cousins or neighbor kids, who was physically punished by his or her parents.

Then, there was all the cooking. Mother swore, with simple German oaths mixed in, as she poked the embers in the old wood-burning range but still managed to make cinnamon rolls and—my favorite— raisin-filled cookies. When I came home—from Kansas State, from the air force, from Mexico City or Chile—there were always pies. One of the last times, she was bewildered and distressed because she could no longer remember how to make them. Heartbroken, I heard her crying in the pantry. But before this, she produced mounds of food. Fried chicken, fried potatoes, pancakes for the family, for threshers, for balers, for the hired men.

Once or twice during the year, when we were all home and I was very small, my mother and father would go off to Kansas City with Aunt Helen and Uncle Walter for a few days' vacation and to oversee the sale of our fattened steers at the stockyards. All of us kids, our cousins, and our friends Dorothy and Donnie Hofmann were then left alone to look after the livestock (the dogs and cats took care of themselves) and sometimes we made hand-cranked frozen ice cream. I cannot remember the *days* when we were left like that; my memory is only of darkness. Long hot summer evenings with June bugs and lightning bugs.

After I had grown up my mother opposed nothing, directly or indirectly, that I planned to do: surely she felt great apprehension but expressed no objection to my enlisting in the air force at nineteen, no objection to being left by her only son to go off to Mexico and then later to California; but in her heart, she must have been disconsolate. She wrote me at least once a week during all those years, telling about the weather, the crops, our relatives and friends, and hoping I was well.

There were lots of letters. Moving house often, I kept few of hers to me, but she—or my father—kept most of mine to them: one hundred and ninety-one in two shoeboxes, to be exact. I found them the day of the farm sale in my father's rolltop desk where he had carefully tied them in ribbons. I brought the letters to California and recently came across them again, in the attic of my present house. Rereading them now, I notice the absence of personal information, not to mention feelings; rather they are brief notes, telling of the weather wherever I happened to be, asking about the weather and crops at home, asking about relatives and friends. Practical, common information.

I came back to the farm several times during my adult years, for brief visits, either alone, with daughter Rebecca, or with wives. Memories of my unforgivably callous behavior remain in my brain: with my life going quite well and no doubt feeling quite grand and giving no advance notice, I came back to the farm from Chile driving a rented car from the Kansas City airport. It was late afternoon. Seeing no one around, I parked the Chrysler (of all things) and walked into the never-locked house. My father's car was not around, my mother not in sight. Seized by an impulse, I rifled through the cupboard to find a box of Special K, a cereal that I knew my father, persuaded by television ads, obsessively consumed every morning. Halfway through the bowl, I looked up to see through the kitchen window my now-old mother bent forward, haltingly making her way up the slope from the cow barn weighted down by a large galvanized pail of milk at the end of each long leathery arm. I rose from the table, intending to help; but then, considering the possible damage to my polished shoes and city clothes, and thinking, moreover, that she was, after all, accustomed to that work, I continued to watch from the window, finished the Special K, and met her at the kitchen door, where joyful tears shone in her eyes at the sight of her only son returned home.

6
Small World

Our farm, before television, suggested a local world like that in the Mother Goose or Br'er Rabbit stories, where a single toad makes his anticipated annual visit and is joyfully recognized by the household. Everyone in our neighborhood knew the blacksmith or the schoolteacher and who lived on the farms in the township. Had there been in the community "a butcher, a baker, a candlestick maker," he or she would have been an intimate as well. It was hard to imagine that radio programs were broadcast from distant cities and not from a nearby town. Even years later, when we got our first television, Uncle Walter used to slap his thigh and talk as if he had a personal relationship with Johnny Carson, a popular late-night talk show performer, "Why, that old Johnny said . . . ," as if Carson were standing among the flour sacks in Cass Kimbrough's store 2 miles away, rather than in a Los Angeles studio.

Uncle Walter, in fact, retained his local view of things into old age. In 1978, when he was over eighty, he came—his first time on an airplane—with his wife, my aunt Helen, to visit us in California. I picked them up at the San Francisco airport and on the way to our house, decided to give them a brief tour of San Francisco. I drove them up Nob Hill and Russian Hill, down steep California and Powell streets, past the towering Bank of America, while they sat nervously in silence. That evening I asked Uncle Walter what he thought of San Francisco. He paused for a bit: "Why, that's pretty rough ground." What might that mean? Then I understood that he had not really taken in the tall buildings or the steep winding streets, but rather, beneath all that entire surface clutter, he saw what a difficult place it would have been to plow and plant.

Along with having a local focus, our perspectives were limited.

None of us had seen the ocean or the Gulf of Mexico; Clay Center, 15 miles away, was an unfamiliar place; Kansas City our London or Paris. When told, we were unable to believe that there were kids in New York City who had never seen a cow. We knew there were lots of "Negroes" in the South and that Chicago and Kansas City were hotbeds of crime, an opinion formed by listening to *G Men* on the radio and hearing the undulating wail of sirens as J. Edgar Hoover and his detectives pursued the likes of John Dillinger, Pretty Boy Floyd, and other daring gangsters.

No one we knew (except for soldiers) had ever seen a foreign country. When Uncle Robert, who had been severely wounded in France during World War I, would affectionately pull me up onto his knee, I longed for him to tell me about the tanks, trenches, and machine guns I'd seen in illustrated histories of the Great War. But he felt more comfortable talking about the farmland he'd seen, comparing it unfavorably to ours, explaining to my father that he didn't think French farmers were up to much, they had only small lots of land. Moreover, no one could understand their "lingo": they had different words for everything.

One day, a distant cousin from a nearby town came with his parents to the farm to visit. We huddled around him on the north porch as he told us of travelling west to Colorado where he had seen the Rocky Mountains. "You can see them a long way off before you get there," he said. "They just rise right up out of the fields and the tallest ones have snow on top even in July." That night at the supper table, my father, who had not seen the mountains but religiously read *The National Geographic*, stood a watermelon on end and, with a butcher's knife, carved upwardly curving spirals to show how cars make their way to the top of Pikes Peak. "You can't drive right straight up the sides," he explained.

In a world regulated by the eastern dawn, western sunset, north winds, and storms from the southwest, natural coordinates were our directional references. People in large cities usually have no sense of east or west, but we talked of the "south forty" or that a neighbor was planting alfalfa "northeast" of the Carter Creek bridge. Once, returning to the farm after having navigated the chaotic street plots of

Casablanca and Mexico City, I was baffled when my father told me that my rifle could be found "upstairs in the northeast corner of the closet in the south bedroom." Although possessing a strong sense of direction, and living in a landscape marked off in uniform square-mile sections, he nevertheless always attached a compass to the dashboard of his cars; I think this was not, however, only a need to know directions, but another indication of his admiration for modernity.

The great inverted bowl of the night sky reinforced a sense of isolation. Outdoors, unless the moon was up to brighten the white branches of cottonwoods down by the creek, when you walked up the rise southeast (!) of the house, the entire landscape was enveloped in blackness unimaginable in our present electrified age. No light anywhere, no other farm close enough for its own flickering yellow lamp to show in the window. No jet planes overhead, no intrusive flicker of satellites skittering along in their tedious terrestrial orbits, just the Milky Way, sometimes the Northern Lights, and always the constellations and a million stars, brighter in my memory than they've ever been since. Returning to the house, we carried pale kerosene lamps to light the dark stairway as we climbed the steps to the bedrooms.

There was no *private* telephone. Our neighbors close by in the surrounding countryside, perhaps a dozen or more, were all on the same "party line." You were supposed to pick up the phone only if it was your "ring," for example "three short and two long," but since all calls rang in all houses and since everyone knew the code (knew who was being called), others on the line, mostly women at home, were inclined to "rubberneck," that is, listen in to calls not their own. "That's Helen's ring," my mother might say, and carefully pick up the receiver. Unless you were very careful, your rubbernecking was revealed by a click and sometimes, after you answered the phone, a succession of clicks might be heard, causing the original caller to shout, "Get off the line!" The party line also served to spread the alarm in case a field or building caught fire. I believe it was five urgent rings that called the neighbors to action. Telephone users were admonished not to use the phone during electrical storms and not to call after 10:00 p.m., except for emergencies, because "the girls in the Central need sleep." We paid $12 a year for the telephone.[1]

Main Street in Green, Kansas, in 1896.

Daylight saving time was an obvious threat to the natural order of things. Resisted during World War I, this national proposal appeared again at the beginning of World War II, shortly after the bombing of Pearl Harbor. It mightily offended many people in our neighborhood, including Grandmother Bauer and Uncles Harry and Paul, who refused to adjust their pocket watches and considered twelve o'-clock—the *real* twelve o'clock—as "God's Time," the only proper time for the midday meal and not something to be tinkered with. I vaguely remember trying to explain, in my eleven-year-old way, to Grandma Bauer one day in the well house that actually, while it was noon where *we* lived, it was a different time in other places, like Colorado, for instance, and even more different in other countries. She set her face against such heretical and useless information, continuing to haul up a basket of butter from the cool depths of the well.

The people I grew up with had only a vague idea of how city people made their living or how they must have prepared themselves for jobs other than farming. Doctors, lawyers, and preachers appeared now and then with satchel or briefcase, but we had no idea how they learned their trade; we knew nothing of college training or professional graduate schools or how you learned to do something other than farming. They were simply accepted as people who must have known what they were up to. Large and distant cities like Topeka or

Wichita, or particularly Kansas City, Missouri, were mysterious and threatening. Before World War II, it was generally assumed that kids my age would be farmers as our parents and their parents and grandparents had been.

Many years later, after I had become a professor at the University of California, I returned home one August to attend a gathering of what remained of our once extended family, in Huntress Park in Clay Center. Strolling past a picnic table laden with pies, iced tea, potato salad, and fried chicken, I overheard behind me an elderly aunt ask Uncle Walter what it was that "Arnold *did* in California." "Why, I'm not sure," Uncle Walter replied. "I think he's some sort of a school dad out there."

—⟫•⟪—

Two miles north of our farm and a bit beyond Fairfield School District #24 was the crossroads curiously called Fact. Local lore has it that an old-timer with naming rights liked the name Wakarusa and when informed that there was already a postal station by this name, is supposed to have remarked, "Is that a fact?" Whatever the truth, the name stuck and the crossroads became our nearest outpost of urban—or at least nonfarm—life. In the 1870s, a wagon hauled by a team of horses brought mail from the Missouri-Pacific railhead to Fact, so that farmers could pick up letters, packages, and later, mail-order catalogues, well before reliable rural free delivery by the post office was established by World War I. By that time, Fact even housed, in succession, two doctors, one called Dr. Bacon, the other Dr. Wheat.[2]

In 1930, the most imposing building in Fact was the limestone United Brethren Church on the northeast corner of the intersection; south, across the road, stood the blacksmith shop. A few steps further along was Cass Kimbrough's high-ceilinged, all-purpose store, which was equipped with a sawdust-packed ice cellar under a trapdoor in the floor and sold items including sugar and flour, tobacco, heads of raw cabbage, binder twine, and pickled fish in wooden barrels. Cass also stocked a few bolts of plain cloth, cans of baked beans, toy balsa-wood airplanes that sold for a dime: the bare essentials. Cass ran the store for fifty-three years, from 1898 to 1951. Outside the store Cass operated a filling station featuring a hand crank that pumped gas into a shoulder-height glass cylinder with gallon markers etched on the side. The gas then flowed by gravity through a hose into the car's tank.

Then, two more houses. One, just behind his store, belonged to the diminutive Cass and his very plump wife, Blanche, a complaining yet benign soul. In the other lived, or was thought to live, a recluse no one ever saw, and certainly I never saw, called Augie Hongsemeier, a bachelor who owned a threshing rig powered by a huge Aultman Taylor tractor. Augie was a powerful man given to drink who died alone and relatively young, in a room in the Tankersley Hotel in Clay Center. The abandoned house in Fact remained dark and silent, the curtains closed, slowly disintegrating, finally caving in.

The United Brethren Church was always packed on Sunday mornings, but in the nonspiritual realm the indispensable blacksmith shop was nearer the center of our universe. If a horse threw a shoe, or a piece of equipment broke down in mid-harvest, or if any number of other problems arose, the nearest help was miles away. That explained why there was almost always a clutch of farmers patiently waiting outside the shop for the blacksmith to work his magic. Following an ancient practice that goes back to Vulcan, the Roman blacksmith of the gods, two successive "smiths" at the Fact crossroads—Fred Easterberg and Clarence Hofmann—spent long smoke-filled days at the charcoal-fired forge heating and then "smiting" the "black" metal.

A good blacksmith offered a variety of arts and services to farmers, from the traditional work of shoeing horses and hardening the steel in plowshares to the repair of all kinds of farm equipment, working with forge and hammer, acetylene and arc welder, to fashion or invent replacement parts. As more cars and tractors appeared, the blacksmith evolved into a mechanic, learning to grind valves, to bore to close tolerance the piston holes in engine blocks, to repair binders and combines. Before 1940, the only power available was a one-cylinder gasoline engine attached to an array of overhead pulleys and belts that drove the trip hammer, the lathe, and drills.

The first blacksmith I vaguely remember was Fred Easterberg, a tall, straight man with a small, well-trimmed moustache. What I didn't know until much later is that he loved music and organized a male chorus out of local farmers who, of course, had no formal musical training. It's hard to imagine a blacksmith, usually associated with trip hammers and welding sparks, leading a choir.

By the time I knew Mr. Easterberg—and his two rather rowdy sons—he had moved to a larger shop in Green, the next step up the urban ladder, and Clarence Hofmann, married to Betty and father of Donnie and Dorothy, had bought the shop and house at Fact. Thereafter, my family became close friends of the Hofmanns, and Donnie, four months older than I, became for a time my best childhood friend . . . and most intense rival. More than once, we rolled in the dirt, wrestling on the gravel path behind the blacksmith shop.

During these years, my father's happiest hours were surely passed in Clarence Hofmann's blacksmith shop. Often, on the way to the shop in the morning—where he'd rapidly become an accomplished designer and builder of farm equipment—my father would drop me at the Fairfield School District #24. After school I'd walk down to the shop, play or fight with Donnie, and wait to go home with my father. But more than once, wrapped up in this work, he'd lose his sense of time and go home without me. Then, responding to my mother's exasperated query, he'd race back to the shop to pick me up, and then return again to milk the cows and feed hogs in the dark.

On another occasion, when I walked from school down to the shop, both Clarence and my father were at work repairing the broken-down springs and brakes of a man driving a DeSoto coupe with a large trunk and Nebraska license plates. The driver had taken the back roads from Nebraska on the way to Fort Riley, and heavily laden with boxes of whisky and gin ("for the troops"), had burned out the clutch. There was no thought, of course, of reporting this to the sheriff, but the bootlegger's misfortune was the source of a good laugh.

By 1930, the five buildings were all that remained of the larger settlement of the late nineteenth century. Of the five, my father far preferred the blacksmith shop, paid no attention to Cass's store, had no truck with Mr. Hongsemeier, and entered the church only for funerals—and, after much coaxing—for our Christmas plays.

During the early days in this part of Kansas, the settlers frequently got together to celebrate the end of the summer harvest. A nearby rural community called Fancy Creek seems to have been the first to do this in our neck of the woods, and one imagines a grassy slope in a small grove of cottonwood and elm trees alongside the creek where a few local farm families gathered, the women tossing their blankets on the ground, hauling out food and drink from cloth-covered hampers, shooing away the ants and bees, while their men stood about waiting for a Sunday meal. Something like this by the end of the nineteenth century came to be called the "Old Settlers Reunion."

A few years later this practice evolved into the small-town "Picnic" that came to be a common feature of the social landscape until the 1960s. The one closest to our farm was 7 miles south in the small town of Green (platted out in 1881 and named for Nehemiah Green, a Kansas governor), which had acquired a 3-acre plot of farmland for a park. By the 1920s, this simple gathering evolved and soon modest livestock shows, the Ferris wheel, carnival barkers and hucksters, games of skill at a nickel a throw, the Fat Lady, two-headed calves, cotton candy and popcorn, and June bugs and mosquitoes all made their appearance.

In the early 1930s, Roosevelt's Works Progress Administration (WPA) put in a concrete dance floor with a covered bandstand that became in the 1950s the main attraction of the picnic-goers. On the rows of benches opposite the bandstand sat the mothers, fanning themselves in the stifling summer heat, cluck-clucking with real or feigned disapproval (and perhaps envy) as their daughters scandalously twirled to the beat of the local band, their skirts flaring up and out, the boys awestruck. My cousin—my favorite cousin—Irma Alexander, daughter of Robert and Ida, was the boldest and prettiest and a fabulous dancer. On a couple of late afternoons before one of the picnics, Irma did her best to teach me to dance. Alas, then—and even now—I feel hopelessly inadequate, klutzy beyond repair, with twinges of envy and insecurity when dance music starts up.

By the 1950s, after the war, cousin Irma and many other teenagers were moving to a faster beat. Out beyond the picnic lights, among the cottonwoods and parked cars, teenaged kids (*some* teenaged kids) enjoyed concealed shots of Southern Comfort in Coca-Cola-filled paper cups, cigarettes, and, sometimes, the sweetest kisses. A Kansas playwright, William Inge, while exaggerating the romantic drama, caught the atmosphere of the small-town picnic in his 1953 play *Picnic,* later made into a movie starring William Holden and Kim Novak.

7
Electricity

My father was an accidental farmer. With his hands and back he worked the land, as he had been born to do, but his heart lay elsewhere. In a different world he may have become an outstanding mechanical or electrical engineer. He learned from the books and articles he acquired how to disassemble and repair car and tractor motors and to design and build farm equipment. He built from his own plans a sawmill that helped us ride out the Depression. He became an artful and creative welder and was able to modify and even invent farm implements.

Even more enthusiastic about electricity than mechanics, my father thought it the greatest thing that ever happened in our neck of the woods. In fact, impatient for the wires to arrive, he built his own wind-driven generator a year before the light poles marched down our driveway. By "built," I mean he wound the armature, carved out the 8-foot-long propeller by hand with a drawknife and rasp from a straight-grained, 2 x 8-inch piece of pine, assembled the frame, and put the entire apparatus up on the ridge of the barn. I want to remember rushing home from school and then, as unlikely as that sounds today, standing silently by his side in a work space off the granary as he rendered the pine into a smooth, symmetrical, and perfectly balanced work of art. No doubt I looked in and dashed out. Whatever the degree of my admiration, on windy days, the generator produced enough electricity to fill a couple of storage batteries, which in turn lit two dim bulbs strung up in the barn. Earlier, my father had found a catalogue where he bought vacuum tubes, resisters, ceramic switches—all kinds of pieces and parts—and built three or four simple battery-powered radios strong enough to capture weak signals from Topeka, the state capital. He enforced silence among us all by tapping a stick as he sat in the living room, ear cocked to the device.

As news of the advancing Rural Electrification Administration (REA) spread, my father read books on electricity and house wiring to prepare himself for the slowly advancing lines of tall, creosoted poles that carried electricity across the wheat fields to the farmsteads. Then the great day arrived when the lines were connected to the house. In my childhood diary, December 20, 1939, age eight, I wrote a single line, "Today we got the electric lights!" That was the last entry until I once again took up my diary in Morocco in 1954.

My father was a strong supporter of REA even though he was filled with scorn for Franklin Roosevelt's New Deal that made it possible. By 1938, power lines reached out from Clay Center, down the country roads—and sometimes, right across open fields as well—to the farms. Alfred Lang, our neighbor to the east, refused electrification of his farm until 1952 precisely because the REA insisted that the power line take a shortcut through his wheat field. My father found Alfred's attitude completely incomprehensible; for him, the glorious arrival of electricity was a thing of beauty that took precedence over everything else.

The incoming high-tension wire led to a yard pole and transformer erected in the very center of the farmstead from which individual wires spread outward to the house, barn, and other outbuildings, creating to my young but apparently precociously aesthetic sensibilities an unsightly clutter of overhead wires. When I innocently asked why we didn't run the wires out of sight, into the back of the house, my father was flabbergasted: the whole point was to show off the new lines; the more visible the better. It has occurred to me in later years that this proud display of modernity or technology, so embedded in the American grain, helps explain why the United States was slow, compared with, say, Western Europe, to place power and telephone lines underground. Even today I am offended by the tangled web of overhead power lines that mars such districts as the elegant Pacific Heights of San Francisco.

As electricity spread throughout the county, my father sent away for more books, catalogues, and manuals on how to wire houses and outbuildings. Beginning in 1939 and into the 1960s, he wired a great many farmhouses, uncounted barns, granaries, and henhouses, not only in the township but also throughout the county. He was an enormously careful craftsman and the REA inspectors came to understand that "if F. W. did the job it's going to be right" and spent little time on their inspections.

My father made very little money in all this. If neighboring farmers came to our house to look at catalogues or inquire about the cost of wire, switchboxes, circuit breakers, or light fixtures, he inevitably would say, "I can get it for you wholesale," when of course, a large part of his profit should normally have come from providing the materials at retail. He charged for jobs at an hourly rate much lower than competitors in town. I don't think anyone ever asked for an estimate; everyone knew the price would be right.

It's hard to imagine now a world, or more specifically one's house and garage, without electricity. Think for a moment that kerosene lamps with their fragile glass and easily broken or blackened chimneys provided the only way to light bedrooms—no reading in bed— or the kitchen and supper table; imagine the same lamps carried shakily (with extreme caution) up the darkened steps to the upstairs rooms, everything outside the house and the outbuildings as dark as pitch. Or consider the lack of refrigeration. Or cooking with a wood-burning stove; the difficulty of food preservation and consequent absence of anything green on the table in the off season; clothes washed by scrub board and dried on the line, outdoors in the summer when my mother and sisters would rush to bring them in when a shower blew up, or indoors—never quite dry—in the freezing winters. There was no electric pump, no pressure system, and no running water. And of course no indoor plumbing or comforting gush of hot or cold water from a handy faucet. We were, in effect, always camping out.

In addition to the now-common electrical appliances in the ordinary American home, there are today some thirty small, many invisible, electric motors. Think of only a few: the clocks and timers, the grinders and mixers, the coffee mill and the Cuisinart, the fans, the hedge trimmers, vacuum cleaners and polishers, the printers, the power drills, saws, sanders . . . all these of course were unknown in the houses that I (and our neighbors) were brought up in, prior to 1939. Small wonder that such disparate modernists as my father and Vladimir Ilyich Ulyanov [Lenin] shared—the only thing they shared!—a passionate enthusiasm for electrification.

All through the early 1940s, weekends and summers, when I was free from grade school, I worked as my father's principal helper by crawling into small spaces, helping string wire, tossing in a perfect arc up from the ground screwdrivers, wire cutters, and drill bits to my father, who clung on climbing spikes to the top of the yard pole. I spent lots of my time in dark and dusty attics waiting for wire to be fished through the walls, and I remember on different occasions hearing on the battery radio downstairs the news about the London blitz, the fall of Bataan, and another time, a few years later, about the death of President Roosevelt, in effect, the man responsible for our electric lights.

As we climbed down the stepladder from the attic at noon, the housewife usually laid out on the dining room table an abundant, cooked dinner—what sophisticated people in Clay Center called lunch—along with pitchers of cool tea brought up from the storm cellar. During the few minutes between the end of the meal and leaping back to work, I saw in the *Topeka Daily Capitol* the curving black arrows on maps that indicated the onslaught of German Panzer divisions across Europe or the marines' bloody landings at Guadalcanal and other Pacific islands held by the "Japs." The war provided terrific geography lessons.

8
The Seasons

Had we been familiar with the illustrations in medieval manuscripts or, say, *The Seasons* as represented in Pieter Bruegel's magnificent sixteenth-century paintings of peasant life in what is now Holland, we might have recognized a certain similarity with our own way of farming in Kansas nearly four centuries later. In the years before electricity came to our farm, we bore a closer resemblance to Bruegel's peasant life than one might think. There were obvious differences but also surprising coincidences. We had, of course, simple farm machinery—McCormick binders, grain drills, and threshing machines that were unimaginable in the flail-wielding cereal culture of Bruegel's lifetime—but we still, like Bruegel's subjects, swung the scythe and cut weeds with the hoe. We used a tractor for heavy work but drove large plodding draft horses for many tasks. One of Bruegel's pictures, *The Return of the Herd*, could—apart from the landscape—easily depict the moving of our cattle from one pasture to another. Bruegel's peasants used hay wagons not much different from ours, drawn by horses similar to ours; like my grandmother, they drew water with wooden buckets, rope and pulley, from a hand-dug well; they lit their lamps with wick and oil and washed themselves with homemade soap, just as my peasant ancestors in Kansas did. They, like us, hunted for winter game—we had better firearms—and heated their peasant dwellings with firewood put up with axe and crosscut saws in the autumn. Alas, my grim Bauer relatives, unlike Bruegel's jolly *Bauern*, did not brew their own beer or stage a joyful festival at harvest's end.

Then, too, our crops and animals—wheat, rye, pigs, fowl, rabbits, and cattle—were very much like those present in Bruegel's landscapes, although we had an advantage in the presence of the new-world potato, a staple, native to the Andes, that his peasants were late to obtain.

In both farming worlds, the natural world was close by. Heifers died giving birth to their first calves, beloved old workhorses gave up the ghost and were unceremoniously hauled off to the glue factory. We were unsentimental about pets, keeping them as mousers or guard dogs, only allowing them in the house if it were below zero and blowing snow. Finally, the rhythms of the agricultural year, located across comparable latitude for Bruegel and for us, were driven by the seasons.

———✦———

Kansas winters, particularly before electricity and running water, tried one's mettle. Some winter days are a cold, brilliant blue, with every detail, even the distant landscape, etched in sharp outline; on other windless days the snow softly falls, piling up high in the pasture, on cedar branches, and on the tops of fence posts. So we'd drag our homemade sled by the rope to the steepest hill behind the barn and slide down all the way to the creek.

But on too many days, the snow comes down at a slant in howling blizzards, sleet breaks off tree limbs, drifts block the road, water in the stock tanks freezes and must be broken for the cattle with an axe. Uncle Walter once made the point that it seemed that there was nothing between Kansas and the North Pole but a barbed-wire fence. The indoor kitchen cistern pump—if you forget to "let the water down"—also freezes; the outhouse becomes a humiliating challenge. There's the daily, round-trip trek to school, and if you don't want to find spoiled muskrats in your trap, the line must be run every day. Two cast-iron stoves: a kitchen range and the large potbellied living room heating stove, both fired with logs from the outdoor woodpile, were meant to provide heat in our house, but actually, we were never warm.

If the corn has been picked there's no remaining outdoor agricultural work, but the animals have to be fed, the cows milked morning and night, the hens—quivering and cranky with cold and pecking your fingers—gently raised from their straw nests and the eggs gathered. The winters also led to a certain family solidarity. My sisters and I played endless card games and star checkers, with my mother and even my father occasionally joining in; we read the *Funk and Wagnall's Standard Dictionary* and created impromptu exams. A few other families had pianos, but except for a pocket harmonica, no one in ours played a musical instrument.

⸺⸺·◆·⸺⸺

The spring day began at dawn with my father's deep, hoarse call for breakfast, chores, and work. In my upstairs feather bed, I'd try to delay the inevitable by thudding single shoes against the wooden floor but eventually I climbed out of bed for a breakfast of fried potatoes and bacon. A single family, with the help of the occasional hired hand, provided the workforce for almost every farm throughout our part of Kansas. This ordinarily meant that the husband and the older boys worked outside in the fields and did the daily chores like milking, feeding chickens, pigs, and cattle, and bringing in firewood, while the mother and girls took care of the house, cooked, canned, cleaned, washed clothes, candled eggs, and churned butter. However, when there were no, or an insufficient number of, male children in a family, the girls were expected to work outside and in the fields, a circumstance, no doubt, that encouraged my independent-minded sisters to flee after finishing high school.

As the spring and early summer go along, weeds grow in the cornrows, and the two-row cultivator is brought out. Because I was too small to haul the heavy leather straps over Molly's and Pete's broad backs or fasten the hame straps, my father fixed the harness over the horses and hitched them to the cultivator. I drove them out from the barn, plodding along, their huge, untrimmed, elephant-like hoofs slapping the earth, to the fields along the creek to cultivate new rows of corn, and at other times, also with Molly and Pete, to mow and rake alfalfa.

Out in the fields, around midday I'd watch for the barn cupola's shadow to fall across the roof, knowing that my mother would soon hang a blue shirt on the clotheline as a signal that it was time to unhitch from the cultivator, bring in the team for water and hay, and have my own dinner, the noonday meal. Our usual meals were breakfast, dinner, and supper, but during the long summer days of harvest or putting up hay, at midafternoon the women brought thick sandwiches of chicken or ham, several cookies, and cool tea out to the fields in wicker hampers.

Before I was old enough to do so, my two sisters did the chores, brought in the firewood, and milked the six cows morning and night. In their early teens they were sent out to "shock" wheat and oats. This meant that they followed the horse-drawn McCormick binder, picking up the bound sheaves, standing them on end, heads up, forming little lean-tos or "shocks" of a dozen bundles, so they might dry in the sun until weeks later when the local threshing machine came around to the farm. My sister Irene later became a career member of the U.S. State Department's diplomatic corps, serving in such places as Moscow, Cairo, Athens, Kabul, Manila, and Frankfurt—a very long way from milking cows in a frozen cow barn in the early dawn light.

Farm kids—my sisters, my cousins on their farms, neighboring kids—all thought of themselves as part of a common enterprise. We lived and worked on *our family's* farm. We knew, and mightily cared about, even as kids, how many bushels to the acre a field produced; we knew the price of wheat at the Greenleaf elevator and how many dozens of eggs or 5-gallon tins of cream we'd have for the weekly passing of the Linn Creamery truck. Any notion that we might be *paid* for our work was unthinkable, never considered. The same was true if we were to help out on a neighbor's farm. The understanding was that, in turn, the neighbor would send over someone when we needed a hand. As the photograph on page 46 demonstrates, in some circumstances, the men of the entire neighborhood might gather 'round to help an unwell fellow farmer bring in the corn harvest. No one kept an accounting of such exchange but there was a general sense of what was right. Our lives were made up of work, that's what we did; that was the purpose of life.

Put another and fancier way, the farm family formed an interdependent, essentially *economic* unit; the *emotional* or *affective* component in the family, although in the best of cases present, was secondary. Marriage ratified a productive unit. Husband and wife needed each

Helping Milo Riek shuck corn. In 1923, forty-seven farmers pitch in to help their ill neighbor, Milo Riek, harvest his corn crop. Alfred Lang is in the first row, far left.

other's labor and they in turn relied on their children's contributions. Each spouse knew that if he or she jumped ship the enterprise was sunk, his or her children's support threatened. This arrangement the kids knew practically from the beginning; it was natural and it was rewarding. We took pride in *our* farm, compared favorably *our* stand of wheat, *our* cattle with the neighbors' fields and herds. In fact, we willingly contributed to the family's income rather than subtract from it. Put in an even fancier way, we *identified* with the family enterprise and did so voluntarily—well, with some early morning prodding—and had no expectation of monetary payment. I wasn't given an "allowance" to buy a Three Musketeers candy bar, but occasionally my father would hand me a nickel at Cass Kimbrough's store so that I might buy one as a special treat.

I remember only that one time, mentioned on page 26, when my mother gave me a good slap on the cheek. Otherwise, I endured no "grounding" nor was I "sent to my room." Let's agree that all families are different and most conceal their secrets, and even, as a famous Russian writer observed, "every unhappy family is unhappy in its own way"; yet, it would seem obvious that there is more tugging-at-the-sleeve, more wheedling, in our present commercial age, and less economic solidarity among families today.

Or is this more old men's talk?

Or is the difference explained by the fact that in the farm families I grew up with, we were all of us—husband, wife, sons, and daughters—part of a common enterprise organized around the inexorable and daily discipline of farmwork? Our routines and responsibilities had long become naturalized; we didn't question the need to care for cattle, chickens, horses, and pigs (moreover, they couldn't live without us). I think that almost from the beginning the kids were treated as mini-adults, *valuable members of the farmwork force*. It was certainly true that among the families in our community, work bent husband and wife to a common, interdependent union.

This was not necessarily, of course, a happy arrangement; it only meant that production took precedence over affection and feelings. In present-day urban life, marriage rests much more on an emotional axis that is often too slender a reed to bear the weight of conflict. If the Kansas farm family was threatened with failure, we called on the Farm Agent for advice on crops; in my current life, we arrange for couples therapy. I do not disapprove of present-day affective culture or long for emotionless toil and sweat but merely describe the difference. Many years ago an intimate friend, brought up in a wealthy Connecticut town, light-years from a Kansas farm, rather idly asked if I'd had a "happy childhood." I was taken aback. Such a question had never occurred to me! Nor do I think anyone ever raised it when I was growing up.

The arrival of the threshing machine in early autumn, drawn at a lordly, 3-mile-an-hour pace by a huge Aultman-Taylor steel-wheeled tractor, was a dramatic occasion. Several of the neighboring farmers and their sons appeared along with their hayracks and teams of horses to help gather up the shocks and pitch them into the rattling, dusty maw of the machine. Other men hauled the threshed grain to the granary in wagons, leveled off to hold almost exactly fifty bushels of wheat. My uncle Gerald pitched the grain from the wagon with such élan that his large aluminum shovel formed a tight flying pattern of wheat in the air, landing almost intact in the granary bin. One harvest day, sitting barefoot and facing my uncle in one end of a wagon nearly emptied of grain, he accidentally drove the blade of the shovel between my toes, opening a bloody gash. I must have howled and I remember him saying—a line I didn't expect, and that must have puzzled me since hardly anyone got divorced—"by the time you're married twice you'll have got over that." Thrice married, I apparently still haven't.

There was another adventure among the threshers and wagons in the field, one afternoon when a sudden storm blew up. We all took cover under the wagons when suddenly there was a deafening crack and a flash of light! The teams of horses were stunned, frozen in their tracks by the million-volt jolt of lightning that struck nearby, and then, recovering in a moment, they bolted, dragging the rattling wagons, stopped only by barbed wire at the field's edge.

At noon the threshers and hired hands came into the house for large piles of fried chicken and bowls of mashed potatoes, tomatoes, and beans from mother's garden, and they often ate a watermelon outside later. If in August there was still ice left in Cass Kimbrough's sawdust-packed icehouse, the men were treated to cold tea. After my sisters left the farm, I became a full-time farmhand at age ten or eleven, working long summer hours in the fields and doing chores year-round. This change came suddenly in the summer of 1941 or 1942. It must have been a warm afternoon, perhaps around two o'clock. My cousin Jerry and I were sitting shirtless in cutoff trousers in a cottonwood grove along the banks of Carter Creek—the one that ran through my grandfather's "home place"—dangling our bare feet into a fishing hole. Across the stubble in an adjoining field, I heard the tractor being turned off and the urgent roar of my father's voice. He was mounted on the combine, the machine that replaced the stationary thresher, harvesting wheat. My sister Irene, up to now the main driver of the steel-lugged John Deere "D" that towed the combine, had become faint in the heat—perhaps it was "that time of month." Whatever the case, she was unceremoniously waved aside and I was summoned as permanent replacement, thus abruptly ending my childhood.

⟶•⟵

In the late autumn when the kernels were hardened and the dried stalks stood bare against new-fallen snow, we picked corn. By that time the cornstalks and the husks rattled to the touch and there was more than a nip of cold in the air. Perhaps the same year that I took over from my sister as the main tractor driver in the wheat fields, I sat alongside my father on the front bench of a wooden-spoke, iron-rimmed wagon hauled along by Pete and Molly, down to the rich bottomland along Fancy Creek to a 15-acre patch of corn. Corn requires better soil than wheat.

After we'd stepped down, having tied the reins to a peg on the wagon, my father demonstrated the correct way to pick the ears. He pulled from his overalls trouser pocket and handed to me a right-hand leather glove with a steel hook riveted into the palm. The picking technique was to grip the ear with the left hand about halfway along the ear. With the hook on the right hand, you ripped the husks aside. A quick snap of the wrist broke the ear from the shank and free of the husk. Your left hand reached for another ear while the right hand threw the picked ear against the bang board—the vertical extension on the wagon's far side—and fell into the wagon. All this is done on the move because the horses are trained to move along at a pace equal to that of the huskers.

When we had filled the wagon with fifty bushels of ears (that would yield twenty-five bushels of shelled corn), we climbed up to the seat. To my surprise and hesitant pride, my father handed *me* the reins. We arrived home at sunset, cold and hungry, I driving the horses, sitting alongside my powerful father, enjoying the manly thrill of working together and the satisfaction of riding atop a creaking wagon filled with yellow ears of corn, soon to be stored to get our cattle and our chickens through the winter. Our farm. My father. Food gathered for our animals—and now perhaps, a supper of newly baked bread, fried bacon, and potatoes.

The urgency of work on the farm, particularly if bad weather threatened, increased the possibility of accidents. There was always a certain danger for a kid working alone behind independent-minded horses, and we'd all heard stories of runaway teams and arms and legs caught in rakes and mowers. Farmers in general were not very safety-conscious; kids, even fairly young kids, were expected to look out for themselves, and even the grown-ups in our community paid little attention to hazards or danger, so there were often accidental injuries and occasional deaths. An abrupt turn by a team of horses pitched George, my father's twelve-year-old brother, over the top of a high, loaded hayrack to hit his head on a post where he died on the spot. This happened long before my time but Grandma Bauer still talked about it.

Another terrible case involved the son of Uncle Gerald and Aunt Irene, a sweet six-year-old kid always known as "Little Robbie," adored by all of us. One winter day Uncle Gerald was grinding milo in a mill powered by an 8-inch-wide belt connected to a tractor standing some 12 or 15 feet away. Little Robbie somehow wandered down unattended from the house to the mill and must have tried to squeeze through the small space between the granary wall and the pulley. The whirling belt caught his elbow and hurled him against the wall. Uncle Gerald gathered up his crushed body, little cowboy boots filling with blood, and carried him up to the house to the arms of his mother. The news quickly spread to our and other farms, and we and nearby neighbors gathered 'round. Little Robbie lay in the kitchen, Aunt Irene twisting a towel, slumped in a heavy chair, inconsolably sobbing.

Other injuries, easily avoidable, were common. With his impatient eye usually cocked at the clock or the weather, my father, in a rush to repair a threshing engine, severely burned his arms as gasoline dripped onto a hot exhaust pipe. Another day, during the years we baled hay, he reached up under the running conveyor belt to unclog the jammed alfalfa. One of the chain links caught his thumb and tore the entire nail backward at a ninety-degree angle. He turned white, sunk to his knees, then, recovered, pressed the nail back in place, and with his good hand, pulled out his red handkerchief, wrapped it around the injured thumb, and we went back to work.

Surely there were differences and disputes with my father, angry and tearful exchanges, but I can't remember any. I don't remember nor can I imagine as a child ever being disrespectful to my father. One tiny exception underlines this truth. One winter evening we drove to Aunt Helen and Uncle Walter's to play cards. I was perhaps fourteen or fifteen, in high school. At the entrance to their house, my father opened the door for Mother and then motioned for me to enter. "After you, Mac," I said, flippantly and thoughtlessly, using a then-vogue high school slang word. He fixed me with a withering glance: "What did you say?" There was no way to respond. I still wince telling this story.

In later years things changed. We had frightful quarrels and rows over politics, socialism, communism, imperialism, and other abstract and unresolvable subjects. But in time, the heat in these discussions faded away.

9
Food and Drink

Why do we acquire the things we do? To feed ourselves might be the first response, for it's easy to see that we expend nearly as much energy in the quest for food as we do for sex. Both, as a rule, are required for our reproduction. Apart from the basic need for nourishment, in lots of societies the kinds of things people eat and the way they eat them derive from traditions or meanings lost in time. We, for example, and most of our neighbors and relatives (often the same thing) followed—unconsciously—the ancient tradition of coloring eggs at Easter that goes back to a Germanic, Anglo-Saxon goddess, Eostre, whose symbol was the implausible egg-laying rabbit. Ham has, of course, a deep religious meaning since eating it—and ordinary pork—marked you as a Christian among the "infidel" Jews and Muslims. There was a more practical explanation on the farm. We slaughtered hogs in late autumn and by spring the cured hams were ready to be taken out of the smoke shed. Closer to the cultural antecedents of my people is the example of the *springerle* cookie. Every Christmas (even though its origin is the Julfest), we brought out the carved rolling pin that pressed several different designs into *springerle* cookie dough, which, when baked, produced a hard, tooth-cracking, and tasteless cookie whose antecedents date back to fifteenth-century Swabia.

I think that when it came to the symbolism of food, practicality and convenience overrode meaning. We ate high-calorie, high-cholesterol, filling and fattening food. We did not taste, sniff, or gravely comment on this or that spice or vintage. Food on the farm was not something you spent much time praising or complaining about or even noticing; it was nourishment, a refueling stop, the caloric intake required for a day's work.

This undoubtedly is a boy's or man's point of view; I'm sure that women—no men except lonely bachelors or widowers cooked—read instructions for canning and exchanged recipes with other women. Indeed, a keen woman's perspective can be found in Mildred Kalish's *Little Heathens*, a delightful account of Iowa farm life and farm food in the 1930s.[1] There, in a contemporary but rather more urbanized rural landscape from the one I describe, the women of the house prepared a wide range of more elaborate vegetable and pastry dishes. I do have fond memories of raisin-filled cookies and simple pies, but except for rare occasions, particularly for canning instructions, I never saw my mother open a cookbook. But then, perhaps I never noticed or perhaps the recipes were etched in her brain. Or maybe her seasoning strategy, as my father not entirely kindly pointed out, really did consist of "a pinch of this and a dab of that," and this was no doubt the judgment of a coarse palate.

Surely the overall aim was to eat food we thought to be healthful (not that it was), served in abundance. We had three meals in the winter: breakfast, the main meal—dinner—at noon, and supper at night. During the long summer days, the women brought "lunch" out to the fields around four o'clock. That meant day after day, some combination of fried eggs, bacon and potatoes, along with home-baked bread and churned butter, sometimes pancakes, for breakfast (shortly after sunrise). A pork chop or ham or sausage and mashed potatoes and perhaps green beans or beets put up in Mason jars, at noon. And then, more meat and potatoes and often fresh milk for supper (after sundown). This, with some addition and subtraction, was the winter regime. Rice and pasta were unknown, or at least they never appeared in our cupboards; we were wheat eaters, and like— well, not *entirely* like—the five rude consumers in Vincent van Gogh's *Potato Eaters*.

Almost all our food was local and seasonal. The glorious arrival of summer added abundant tomatoes, lettuce, corn on the cob, peas, and beans. Week-old chicks raised in the brooder house during the early spring were culled as they matured, the pullets or layers sorted out to produce eggs for sale, the roosters destined for slaughter (be-headed and plucked) ending up fried in high piles on the dining room table. Now and then, my father found that someone had a good orchard crop and would bring home a wicker bushel basket of peaches or plums. We'd eat our fill until they began to go soft and mother would can the rest. In the late summer, trucks appeared heaped with watermelons from Sand Springs near Abilene. My father was persuaded they had a salutary effect on the kidneys and was pleased to buy several for a dime apiece. There was no fresh fruit out of season with the exception of bananas—which, thanks to United Fruit Company's "Great White Fleet" and its advanced refrigeration methods, might be found even on the small, dry, grocery store shelves in Clay Center: yet another salutary advantage of imperialism.

Drought or not, we grew our own garden produce. The cistern that depended on roof runoff dried up, but the dug well and windmill continued to provide enough water for daily use, including drinking water. Women tended the gardens and carried buckets of water for irrigation. When we "went visiting" we often carried along whatever surplus vegetables we had for the neighbors.

There were rare trips to town to buy coffee, sugar, tea, the odd spice or sweet. Now and then we were treated to a black walnut ice cream cone on Saturday nights in Clay Center. Apart from such delicacies, we had little need to go either to Clay Center or the smaller town of Green, 7 miles to the south, for store-bought food.

In the late fall, after the wheat and corn harvests were in, my father, Uncle Gerald, and two or three strong lads from neighboring farms assembled at Grandfather Bauer's "home place" for the annual slaughter. This began early in the morning when the men rounded up four or five large, usually white, squealing hogs in a penned-off section of the barn under a rope and pulley attached to an overhead beam. With a deft move, one of the more daring young men—hogs have sharp teeth and can be dangerous when cornered—tied the back legs together while another man quickly hoisted the writhing hog's body into the air. At that point, the hired butcher, a nearby neighbor, stepped forward to slit the pig's throat, its blood gushing into a wide, enameled pail, later to find its way into blood sausage. The men lifted the carcass onto a sturdy table outside the pen and the butcher, with long knives and meat saws, carved up the animal into hams and slabs of bacon for curing in the smokehouse, loin for chops, random slices and pieces for sausage and for canning in Mason jars, intestines set aside for sausage casings, feet sawed off for pickling, head meat scooped out (eyes discarded) and cooked to make a substance called "head cheese," catnip to the adults, repellent to me. We usually had artery-clogging fried liver for supper on butchering days.

This process was repeated, as I've said, four or five times in the course of a few days, creating a small mountain of joints, loose slabs of meat, and offal. Inside the big house the women, always including my mother and Aunt Helen and organized by my severe, pious, unsmiling grandmother Nettie—grey hair pulled back into a tight bun—trimmed thick sections of fat for rendering into snow-white lard, chopped chunks of lesser cuts into a large, hand-turned sausage grinder mounted on a sturdy board, then dumped the slick mass into a wooden press that extruded the meat mixed with garden-grown spices into long tubes pinched off into 6-inch segments—one day to become excellent sausage. The entire business, from slaughter to sausage, lasted for I forget how many days. Not an event for the squeamish.

I have the notion that the slaughter of steers took place in the spring; I'm sure it was separate from hogs. Anyway, in both cases we hired a skilled butcher, usually a neighbor, who brought the tools of his trade—large, sharp, heavy knives and saws, along with a .22-caliber rifle. Aiming at a point created by drawing an imaginary X from opposite horn to eye, he always managed to fell the animal with a single shot. Watching this deadeye marksmanship more than once from behind a wooden fence, I was mightily impressed. In the absence of electricity, we cooked and canned the meat in Mason jars and cured by smoke the ham and bacon.

Apart from slaughtering farm animals, we obtained our other fundamental food in a way not too different from the exchange between miller and peasant in fourteenth-century France. Every two or three months we hauled six 60-pound sacks of wheat up to the Clyde mill and came home with five sacks of pure white flour from which mother made loaves and loaves of bread, endless pies, and cookies. Just as in the feudal era, the miller kept the extra sack for the milling charge. At home we stored the flour in the pantry (it took a long time for me to see the "pan"—Latin *panis* = bread—in pantry) made mouse-free by my father, who nailed aluminum strips over the wooden seams.

⟶•⟵

The subject of drink begins with water, of which we had two sources: the cistern, a step or two outside the kitchen door, and a dug well several hundred yards west of the house in the pasture. The cistern received runoff from the shingled roof; obviously whatever was on the roof—leaves, dust, bird droppings—also found its way onto the gutters and then through rude charcoal filters into the cistern. We never drank this water, but because it was "soft," we used it for cleaning, washing dishes, and watering plants. Rusty, rectangular tin cups, attached to a long, linked-chain rotary device turned by hand, dipped far down into the cistern to bring up the water to the outdoor platform; inside the house, a cast-iron hand pump raised water during the hard-freezing winters. During the summer, harmless snakes and frogs hung out in the cool, damp overflow along the edge of the cistern.

It's hard to overestimate the importance of drinking water for the first immigrants into Clay County and even harder to imagine how the solution for water was accomplished. Innumerable letters from early pioneer women tell of the search for water; one reports that "we had men out in every direction . . . they traveled forty or fifty miles but found none."[2] Two of the three surviving letters from the homesteading Alexanders to their relatives left behind in Hessen-Cassel emphasize the problem of water. Within the first months of arrival in Kansas, the more touchingly optimistic of the two letters assures the old-world cousin, "*Es gibt gutes Wasser in diesem Land*" (the water in this land is good). I presume they loaded their wagons in Kansas City with barrels or ceramic containers of water, and then, I presume again, that if, creaking westward, the pioneers had not captured rainwater, they must have boiled the clearer creek or river water.

But for settlement—for the long term—wells became not only urgent but essential for survival. First, a likely source of underground water had to be found. When I was growing up, a "water witcher" was not an unfamiliar character; indeed, my uncle Walter had a certain fame—scoffed at by my father—for finding water. The witcher cut a Y-shaped branch, or "divining rod," from a willow or hazel tree and held the branch in front of him by the upper fork while carefully walking over what he considered a likely source. When the stem of the branch turned down—Uncle Walter claimed it actually twisted in your hands—the presence of underground water was announced. The witchers, the skeptics noticed, often chose a damp or marshy swale to improve their chances of success.

If a proper source of water were found, witchers or not, the hard work began by digging a hole of a diameter adequate for at least two men to work with spades and shovels excavating down to the water table. Above, at ground level, one or two men hauled up the stone and dirt in a large bucket. If water of apparently sufficient volume appeared, rocks or stones appropriate for lining the well were somehow found and carted to the wellhead. These were laid up, without mortar, in such a way as to keep the well from caving in, no small accomplishment. The well diggers brought along their old-world arts.

The first notice I've found of a *drilled* well was near Green in 1871. Presumably, some sort of horse-powered whim, or winch mechanism, was employed. The account claims that the well reached a depth of 101 feet with 30 feet of water.[3] Several hundred yards west of our house near the banks of Fancy Creek, the first settlers found water and dug a well some 6 feet in diameter and perhaps 30 to 40 feet deep and lined it with limestone rocks. The water level, even during the great drought of the 1930s, held fast at about 30 feet. A pipe with a coarse filter in the submerged end rose to the well's platform, where one opened a tap for drinking water and for a livestock tank.

Bringing the water up from the well required either a bucket and rope or a windmill, and happily, windmills arrived almost with the first settlers. Already in 1879, one report reads, "windmills dot the prairies of Kansas."[4] Factories sprung up locally in the larger towns but by the 1890s, a Chicago-built windmill and pump became dominant in the countryside; its sheet-metal rudder with its red-painted "Aermotor" logo provided an irresistible target for boys with their .22-caliber rifles hunting in the area.

In order to bring the water closer to the house, my father, with the help of a team of mules and a couple of hired hands, ran a pipe from the windmill to a steel standpipe for pressure, and then to the house where a spigot provided cool, clear, and apparently safe drinking water. Until electricity brought better motors and pumps, most other families lugged buckets of water long distances from the windmill.

⸺•⋅⋅⸺

When we felt thirst, we thought water. In hot weather it was kept in a ceramic crock in the cellar. Canned or bottled soft drinks were unknown, but I can recall the heady taste of a root beer float in Clay Center on a Saturday night. Before refrigerators, we got lake ice packed in sawdust from Cass Kimbrough's store. A thin and spindly man, he brought up with his tongs the heavy, rough-hewn blocks and, tottering, flung them at our feet on the plank-board floor. Once the blocks were placed in our insulated icebox at home, we chipped off slivers to cool iced tea, and—when we had lemons—made lemonade, a rare treat. After the magical electric lines arrived in 1939, we quickly got our first refrigerator and soon thereafter, a hot plate and toaster.

No one in my immediate family drank alcohol, or at least, very rarely. Abstinence from alcohol was not so much a matter of principle as the fact that there was none around, or at least there was no legal alcohol to be had apart from home-brewed beer or the insipid and watery, less-than-3.2-percent tap beer sold in the Idle Hour pool hall in Clay Center. Kansas, late home to Carrie Nation the crusading temperance warrior, was the first state to prohibit the consumption of all alcoholic drink (in 1881) and the last to permit the sale of alcohol by drink "on the premises" (in 1987). During the years 1971–1975, in fact, it was hypothetically *illegal* to serve alcohol in jets *flying over* Kansas or on passenger trains rumbling across the parched landscape, but the law was rarely, if ever, enforced.

Prohibition did not, of course, stop people from drinking. My father's two younger brothers, Harry and "Hook" (Paul), both with a decided taste for alcohol, found it tempting and easy to drive over the state line to Nebraska or Missouri, both "wet" states, and bring back raw whisky and gallon jugs of cheap California wine. Grandmother Nettie, despite her severe, joyless Protestant faith, looked the other way when her youngest and coddled sons came home plastered. Once, when Father and I were standing in the home-place yard, Hook and Harry drove in, having just returned from a whisky run to Nebraska. They hopped out of their car in high spirits, spied a couple of Rhode Island Red hens, and gave chase, drunkenly reeling, tumbling, laughing like mad at their own antics. Surprised, bewildered, and maybe alarmed, I remember turning to my father for explanation. But explanation was beneath him, not, I later learned, because he was opposed to the odd drink, but because it must have seemed a waste of time.

A far more serious matter occurred when Uncle Frank (who was actually my great-uncle on my mother's side) acquired a small still that he set up in the barn and began to sell jars of coarse whisky to a small number of disreputable neighbors. Worse, he sold on credit, and the attempt to collect payment on an illegal substance attracted the attention of federal agents. "I looked through these cracks in the barn door," Uncle Frank later told me—I must have been open-mouthed and slightly frightened, since we were standing in the very place where the still had been—"when I saw these two men, all dressed up in suits and ties, drive up to the house and then come right up here. I had a rifle and I could have taken a shot at them." Instead, he was sentenced to two years in Leavenworth Federal Prison, an experience Uncle Frank always happily described as "cooking for the prisoners." I believe my father said he was let out early for good behavior.

When I was seven or eight, Uncle Frank lived as a widower on a farm just a mile directly east of our place. He must have died in the 1940s, so I knew him only slightly, but there were lots of stories about him, including those told by my father with a kind of wry admiration despite his general disapproval of his in-law's reckless ways. There was the Saturday night bath scene, for example. Uncle Frank was scrubbing himself in a galvanized steel bathtub in the middle of his kitchen. He heated bathwater in steaming pots on the wood-burning stove and no doubt slopped some onto the linoleum floor. When an unanticipated car drove up to the house, dear Uncle Frank leapt up, stark naked of course, and slipped and fell across the tub, cracking several ribs. The kindly, visiting farm couple pushed open the screen door, gathered him up in a towel, and drove the 15 miles to the Clay Center Community Hospital.

10
Diversions

Games and play seem to be embedded in our DNA. Etymologically, the word for "game" and, by extension, "to play" goes back to Old High German *gamen*, suggesting mirth, fun, and games. So apparently, we were *supposed* to have fun, and I think it's fair to say that with the exception perhaps of Grandma Nettie, we often did. Except for solitaire—also called patience—and games invented by single and bored boys and girls, all of our card and board games as well as outdoor games were terribly simple and involved competition with other human beings.

In the spring when wildflowers came out, a number of kids, mostly our cousins, would come over in the early evening to go "May-basketing." That meant gathering little basketfuls of wildflowers, creeping down the lane to other farms, hanging the flowers on the doorknob with a little knock, and then quickly scattering to hide behind trees or outbuildings to watch the surprised and delighted look on the face of the housewife. It's hard to imagine anything more innocent or less dramatic but I remember the little thrills of success.

Older kids and even young adults prowled the countryside on Halloween night. Sometimes, my father would drive us around the morning after, pointing out the dangling wagons and buggies and toppled outhouses on several farms. Everyone, too, heard stories about Allie, mischievous wife of neighbor Alfred Lang, who loved to terrorize young people who came out on Halloween. On one occasion, as the tricksters crept down the long driveway toward the Langs' house on the night of a waning moon, she emerged from a gloomy grove of cottonwood trees, wrapped in a fluttering white sheet, emitting a terrible moan. The young intruders turned heel and fled up the driveway, but eventually gathering courage and suspecting one more trick from the devilish Allie, returned to knock at the kitchen door to inquire slyly whether she might be found in the house. "Of course," Alfred answered, "she's asleep." Still skeptical, he led them to the conjugal bed where Allie, moments before, had slipped in the back door and tucked herself, fully dressed, under the covers.

Another peculiar business was the "chivaree." The first night after a couple married, the farm neighbors, grown-ups and kids, assembled at the newlyweds' darkened house and made a terrific din with pots and pans until the couple appeared at the upstairs bedroom window. Kerosene lamps came on; the new bride and groom descended to the dining room and invited everyone in for a substantial meal they'd previously laid out. These were jolly occasions with good-humored kidding and horsing about. It never occurred to me, of course, to wonder what the newlyweds were doing upstairs with the lights out. Actually, by the time I was eight or nine, just before the war, the custom of the chivaree was ending. I vaguely remember one or two.

From an early age, we kids played cards among ourselves and occasionally with cousins and neighbors. The most primitive games were War, Lazy Eight, and Go Fish, graduating to Pitch, a simple, engaging, and good-humored card game. More sophisticated people, mainly in town, played pinochle; I'm sure that no one we knew had heard of bridge. During the slack winter months we became devoted to Chinese checkers. My father made the star checkerboard by boring holes in a foot-square of scrap plywood, sanding and painting, and then gluing a hardwood border around the four sides to retain the marbles. The game captivated us for several months, maybe years. By the light of the Coleman or kerosene lights we read or played cards, star checkers, or ordinary checkers on the round dining room table. By the late 1930s, we got Monopoly and Scrabble as Christmas presents.

At Christmastime, and sometimes for birthdays, neighbors and family exchanged presents among themselves, many drawn from the farm itself, such as jars of jam and jelly; hard, German-style cookies; and smoked hams. My most memorable Christmas gift was a red bicycle that cost $24, a fortune at the time. My sisters pushed the bike up the small grade south of the house and pushed me off downhill as I struggled to find my balance. I don't know how many times I landed in a heap at the bottom but then eventually managed to wobble along and finally ride off. I longed for pavement, any kind of pavement, some kind of sidewalk, to ride on.

Another day my father returned from town and surprised me with an unwrapped gift from heaven in the form of a flat, yellow leather baseball mitt with no webbing and hardly any padding; it was, in fact, a kind of thin leather hand glove. It cost $1. I remember feeling, along with joy, a certain remorse and selfishness at this unexpected expense, particularly since there was no birthday or holiday to justify it. After the electricity and the war came and the economy was looking up, my father bought a small electric train, mounting the tracks on a plywood base. For the first time—it was the Christmas of 1939—we had electric lights strung on a cedar tree cut from the little grove just south of the house.

My father was able to invent remarkable toys that he'd do out of sight in his shop and then, once finished, spring them on me. One was a small ship, made of tin sheets, hammered out and soldered to prevent leaks, powered by a tiny steam boiler—that he also invented—fired by a kerosene-soaked wick that somehow propelled the vessel across the stock tank, the largest body of water on the farm. Another time, he wound two small, battery-powered electrical armatures and connected these to keys and contact points that, when joined by wires, allowed Donnie Hofmann and me to tap out Morse code messages to each other from different rooms. This device is on a shelf in the kitchen of my house. Perhaps I should say, on the *north* wall of the kitchen.

As far as sports went, work left little time for outdoor play, a situation aggravated by my being a single child once my older sisters had gone off to high school. The closest potential playmate was 2 miles away. So I invented solitary games, such as throwing a baseball onto the high barn roof to catch it as it came rolling down, or pitching horseshoes, not against an opponent but in competition with myself. I kept track of ringers per 100 tosses. For several months, maybe years, I practiced this game after school in a cottonwood grove, eventually working up to 25 or 30 percent ringers: not bad for an amateur (professionals are up there in the 95th to 96th percentile).

On Sundays, local farmers organized baseball games, played in work shoes and overalls, wherever a level patch of prairie-grass pasture could be found. Dirt-filled flour sacks served as bases, and outfielders chasing foul balls occasionally ran headlong into barbed-wire fences. Because lots of people still lived on farms, there were enough young men to put together teams in most local townships, and they played the games with high interest and energy. My father was a pretty good catcher, my uncle Gerald an accomplished left-handed hitter. These games must have begun around World War I and came to an end by 1941 as young men were drafted into the army and others left to work in war industries. Baseball was the only organized sport farm kids played or saw; football and basketball, not to mention tennis and golf, were games played only in towns and colleges. Although fairly athletic, I never made the first-string high school football or basketball teams.

As for attending, watching, or listening to professional games, there was, of course, no television, but by the late 1930s or early 40s, farm families had battery-powered radios or car radios. Surprisingly, boxing was popular. We were glued to the radio for the June 1941 match between the great "Negro" Joe Lewis, heavy-weight champion of the world, and his challenger, Billy Conn, "The Pittsburgh Kid." Why did I root for Billy Conn? Thoughtless, conventional racism?

Lots of people listened to baseball games. The team closest to us, the only team west of the Mississippi and the only big-league team within reach of our radio, was the St. Louis Cardinals, and so if anyone in our neck of the woods found the time and had a decent radio, he listened to the broadcasts of that team. I have clear memories of the agonizing effort of straining to capture the wavering signal of the simulated Cardinals broadcast on sultry summer nights when, unknown by me until much later, the announcer was not actually present at road games but read the action from a Western Union tape, making up the crowd noise or the crack of the bat. The Cardinals are still the only team I follow.

Perhaps many kids, if they spend lots of time alone, are more given to daydreaming and imagination than a young person immersed in company, hanging out with his "peer group." At maybe eleven or twelve, working in the fields, driving horses or tractors, I imagined warring flotillas (I didn't use that word) of destroyers, cruisers, and P.T. boats engaging in fierce conflict with the "Jap" and Nazi fleets on Carter and Fancy creeks, which were in my imagination broad rivers and estuaries, not muddy and reed-filled streams.

Upstairs at night in the dark bedroom, I saw myself flying a Spitfire in the Royal Air Force intercepting Messerschmitt fighter planes and shooting down Heinkel and Stuka bombers in the Battle of Britain. All this, of course, is what lots of kids do. But maybe a difference is that I always flew or fought alone. A strong emotion that lasted a long time was loneliness; perhaps the open landscape or the distant horizon, unobstructed by buildings or mountains, or the broad night sky and the menacing, dancing fire of the Northern Lights, reinforced this sense of isolation.

11
Attitudes

I have a friend whose Ohio parents were Communists, the large *C* meaning that they were members of the Party USA. And this meant that around the kitchen table with his parents and their friends, there was intense talk about socialism and Marxism, injustice, workers and labor unions, Henry Wallace, and other political ideas.

On the farm, as one might imagine, there was much less talk of politics. That subject, along with, say, religion, was beyond my mother's interests and my father must have basically thought that political talk generally was a waste of time because it interfered with the workday. He naturally loathed communism and socialism, but they were never discussed, except later, during the McCarthy years. He limited his thoughts on Roosevelt's New Deal to irritated muttering.

William Jennings Bryan, the turn-of-the-century Populist leader and presidential candidate, however, came up more than once. My father had learned and committed to memory several lines of William Jennings Bryan's "Cross of Gold" speech to the Democratic National Convention held in Chicago in 1896. Now and then he'd quote Bryan with unusual fervor and, I'd like to think, without missing a beat. But no doubt the lines were not exactly as the Great Commoner put it in Chicago: "The great cities are in favor of the gold standard. I tell you that the great cities rest upon these broad and fertile prairies. Burn down your cities and leave our farms and your cities will spring up again like magic. But destroy our farms and grass will grow in the streets of every city in the country." Then the moving finale: "You shall not press down upon the brow of labor this crown of thorns. You shall not crucify mankind on a cross of gold!"

Writing this now, it does seem unusual that we heard these words addressed to us over the supper table. Did I and my sisters quietly put down our knives and forks and listen without sidelong glances? Was my mother embarrassed? Did he really subscribe to the sentiment disclosed in these lines? Or did they simply reveal an appreciation of the spoken word? Reading them aloud today gives me a chill down the spine. My father must have agreed with Bryan on the importance of farms but I don't think he felt much kinship with laboring men. I was too young at the time to raise a question and, in later years in conversation with my father, I never explored these childhood memories.

The other main public figure my father admired—more so in fact than Bryan—was Bryan's most severe and articulate critic, William Allen White, the editor of the small-town Kansas newspaper the *Emporia Gazette*. In an editorial a few weeks after Bryan's great speech, White responded with a scathing editorial, "What's the Matter with Kansas," ridiculing Bryan's Populism. White had an eloquent, sober, down-home manner that not only disapproved of Bryan's politics (including the Cross of Gold speech) but also took a fiercely strong stand against the Ku Klux Klan that flourished for a few years in Kansas in the 1920s. My father would certainly have admired White for that position.

As for ethnic heritage, even though my father, the son and grandson of German immigrants, mainly spoke German before going to school, German and Germany soon became alien to him. Even before the beginning of World War II, my father wagged his head in grim disapproval of Hitler, and of course a bit later, the "Japs," although here, I think, he was as scornful of their shoddy goods as of their imperial ambitions.

My mother's Lutheran baptism was recorded and printed in German but her connection to German culture was limited to a few swear words such as *Mein Gott* and *Himmel*. We were, or should be, Americans all the way through, and it was thought right and proper that Uncle Robert and Bill Riechers and other farm kids should go off to fight the Germans in 1917 as other uncles and cousins would do in 1942. I've never felt any affinity for things German, and I remain ignorant, not proudly so, even of Germany's great writers.

I don't believe you could apply the term "racist" to my father or to the people on the surrounding farms, in part because they had little experience with nonwhites and consequently little opportunity to feel or express ethnic disdain. Asians, "Negroes," or Mexicans were rarely, if ever, seen in the flesh on the farms in our neighborhood; there was not a single one among the 300 students in the Clay County Community High School. My father was aware of, and occasionally mentioned as historically interesting, the small black farming town of Nicodemus some 150 miles to the west that had been founded in 1877 by former slaves from Kentucky seeking free soil, and of course, legendary jazz musicians such as Count Basie and Charlie Parker would seem today only a stone's throw away in Kansas City (Missouri). But neither the fame of Nicodemus farmers nor the jazz greats impinged on our consciousness. "Negroes," it was thought, lived in the South; Asians were far away. In what now seems improbable talk, I'd heard that Mexican railway workers, accidentally scattering seeds, were responsible for the wild marijuana plants that flourished in the pastures. I imagine that my parents and our neighbors saw Mexicans, if they saw them at all, in terms of the common stereotype: simple, smiling, perhaps dangerous, and in any case, of scant relevance to their lives.

My people in rural Kansas could only glimpse at a distance people of a different ethnicity. They were all very abstract figures, more rarities than objects of disapproval, appearing only in stories and pictures in *Look* or *Life* magazine. But had a "Chinaman" or "Negro" or Mexican actually appeared at our doorstep, he or she would certainly have been treated with curiosity, maybe suspicion, but also with ordinary human respect. My father was an egalitarian, unawed by the local rich, compassionate toward the poor, but scornful and intolerant of sloth or excuses. He believed in "stick-to-it-ive-ness," a quality, as he now and then pointed out, I lacked.

My first experience with a real "Negro," I believe, was during my first year in high school when the students were asked to go door-to-door in Clay Center to raise money by selling Christmas seals. On my assigned route across the tracks, I knocked at the door of a run-down house and was taken aback when an old, thin, black man with short grey hair came to the door. "Why son," he said, "I ain't got no money, I'm poorer than skimmed piss."

<hr />

Just to the north of us, in the next township, was a settlement of Irish farmers. I notice that I call them "Irish" farmers while I don't refer to "Swedish" or "German" farmers. Did we think of them as less "American"? Perhaps they had come more recently? In any case, the "Irish" were known to have a few jolts of whisky, and once or twice on a Sunday morning we'd see a car in a ditch with the driver slumped over the steering wheel, sleeping off the effects of the previous night. Because of this reputation, Uncle Walter (who was known to have a drink now and then himself) described them as "pretty rough people."

Then too, in the mosaic of different, mainly Protestant, nationalities that had settled northeast Kansas, the only Catholics were Irish and consequently they came under a double suspicion. When one of her grandsons contemplated marriage with a Catholic girl, Aunt Helen objected, but she finally came around to approve the relationship by pointing out that although it was true the girl was Catholic, "she wasn't a very good Catholic."

My father got along famously with the Irish. We occasionally hired a thirtyish, live-wire bachelor, fond of drink and dance, called Eldred O'Brien as a live-in hired hand. We also baled hay for Irish farmers and my father wired many of their houses and installed electricity in the Catholic church. This structure, along with the priest's house and a gasoline station, formed the crossroads known as Kimeo.

The Kimeo Catholic Church, in my youthful gaze a *huge* limestone building, was, next to the grain elevators, the tallest edifice around, towering above the low, rolling countryside like a Chartres of the wheat fields. When I returned forty years later it had become much, much smaller. Here too, in wiring this building, I was my father's principal helper. We were given a tiny taste of sacramental wine in the cellar, fed at noon in the parish house, and then, to my everlasting (as you can see) surprise, Father Brown took my arm. We climbed the stairs and walked together into his study, a dark, wood-paneled room. There was an alarming painting of Jesus, his Sacred Heart exposed in vivid red, on the wall. Father Brown pulled out a desk drawer, opened an envelope, and gave me a single dollar bill for being such a good boy working with my father and all. What a great man!

During those same days, I was mightily impressed when, one day, Father Brown was required to demonstrate his aplomb in the midst of disquieting circumstances. While we were engaged in wiring the church, Dick Kimbrough, a large and rotund guy known by everyone as "The Man Who Was Divorced," was hired to paint the rooms on either side of the altar. One morning while we were installing electrical outlets in the nave, we noticed Father Brown apparently pointing out some question or detail in the painting of one room. He then set out at a brisk pace across the front of the church for the opposite room with Dick, full stride, in close pursuit. Crossing the altar, Father Brown dipped in a quick genuflect. Unable to brake, Dick pitched his ample body directly over the back and shoulders of the astonished priest, both ending up in a tangle on the floor. Without a word or smile from either man, Father Brown dusted himself off, gathered his dignity, and continued on.

Jewish people were loosely associated with the city—generally with Kansas City and specifically with the building materials and iron yard of the Sonken Galamba Company where my father, if the weather at home didn't allow him to work, might accompany a truckload of cattle destined for the stockyards to pick up a few lengths of angle and channel iron for various projects. My father explained, "I always like to have some iron around." Over supper after these excursions, there was usually a bit of muttered disapproval about the low prices for cattle compared with how much we paid to "those gougers." Anti-Semitism, I suppose, was a latent, underlying prejudice, but again, had a Jew appeared at the farm, my father would have been far more interested in his goods than in his ethnicity and would likely have remarked on what an enterprising fellow he was.

I learned early in life that sex was an inappropriate subject for public—or even private—discussion and kept firmly underground, apart from Uncle Walter's occasional snigger. One day—I must have been nine or ten—waiting for my father to descend from the attic for the noonday meal in the Girardy house that we were wiring, I idly turned the pages of two or three magazines—or perhaps they were catalogues—in the rack next to my chair. Many pages were partly shredded, the illustrations or ads clipped out. Mrs. Girardy, my father later explained, intercepted the publications before her husband had a chance to look at them and clipped out overly stimulating pictures such as, I now imagine, a woman with bare arms exposed or a full-figured milkmaid.

I doubt, but cannot know, whether our parents talked very much between themselves, if at all, about sex, and that topic certainly did not intrude in our daily life. Perhaps they believed that observing the care and breeding of a multitude of farm animals and, for that matter, given the presence of midwives and home births, we'd all eventually get it. Or, more likely, parents didn't know *how* to talk about sex, didn't want to open that Pandora's box, with their kids.

My sister Lucille told me, years after the event, that when first menses appeared, she stood distressed and bewildered on the stairway landing of our house and indicated a need for assistance. My mother quickly appeared at the bottom of the stairs, and without a word, then or later, tossed up a sanitary napkin. I don't think my family was unusual in this. Talk of sex wasn't necessarily taboo; it was just unbearably awkward and embarrassing.

Adolescents on their own, impatiently waiting, let's say, for their parents in the family car on a Saturday night in Clay Center, no doubt engaged in more than one giggling or boasting discussion. In my case, the whole business was very mysterious. The closest I got to sexual titillation as a young adolescent was the lingerie section of the Sears & Roebuck catalogue, whose petticoat and girdle ads were not exactly Victoria's Secret, but still, as I recall, produced some high-in-the-chest heavy breathing.

Aunt Helen, an apparently enthusiastic sexual partner of Uncle Walter before marriage, later in life became disapproving of all such activity. Our neighbor, Alfred Lang, teased me about girls and expressed hope that one day I might take up with a "smooth-legged schoolmarm." Although it wasn't a topic of conversation, I have no doubt that men and women and many adolescents in our township—alas, not I—discovered the joys of sex, some perhaps tenderly, others abruptly. I'm pretty sure my mother never heard the word "homosexual" in her entire life, and if she had, I don't think she could have imagined such a relationship. Once, returning from California in the 1970s, I remember seeing a photograph of some distant cousins on Aunt Helen's buffet and asked whether "Ronald," who looked like the very essence of a San Francisco gay man in the photograph, had ever married. "Oh, not yet," she said, and then added, "You know, he was always something of a sissy."

On another occasion, around age nine or ten, I came home from school and Mother, flour on her apron, was patting out raisin-filled cookies on her marble board.

"Imogene Stetnisch," I announced, "told me that if Donnie Bolin's mother hadn't fucked with his father, Donnie wouldn't be here." I'd never heard that verb before Imogene used it, nor, I think, had my mother.

"What do you mean?" she asked.

"You know," I explained, "like what bulls do to cows."

"You have to talk to your father about these things," she said, which, of course, I never did.

12
Dying at Home

In my grandparents' generation, old people usually died at home. With no health insurance, long hospital stays or a hospice were—except for the well-off—prohibitively expensive. My mother lived her last few days in a Lutheran hospice; by that time, in 1975, there was simply no family to take care of her. Before, given the large families, there was usually an abundance of sons and daughters around to care for their parents in their final years. Three of my four grandparents died in their own beds.

On December 14, 1939, a few days before the miracle of electricity came to the home place, my paternal grandfather, William Jakob Bauer, lay dying by the light of Coleman and kerosene lanterns in the big house on the home place. All of the extended family—the five surviving sons and Aunt Helen, and their families, plus all of us grandkids—gathered on the farm. Inside the house, dressed in Sunday best, the adults joined in as best they could, as Grandma Nettie belted out on the piano "The Old Rugged Cross" and other solemn hymns. Outside the house, muffled up against the cold, the grandchildren scattered out among the several outbuildings to play hide-and-seek and wait for the report that Grandpa had emitted the "death rattle," which we imagined we'd be able to hear, even outdoors. That night he "passed away" (with no death rattle as far as we knew), and the next day his unembalmed body, dressed in his Sunday best, lay in his bed off the living room as neighbors and relatives from near and far came "to pay their respects."

A procession of cars then followed the hearse and casket, brought out from Clay Center by the grimly named "undertaker," for burial in the township's Schaubel Cemetery, a half-mile away on an acre that once belonged to the Lang farm. After that, everyone returned to the house for a huge spread of food, coffee, and tea and to talk quietly, mainly about weather and crops. Shortly thereafter, Grandma bought a small house in Clay Center and moved into town, leaving my uncle Gerald and aunt Irene to manage the home place.

My maternal grandfather, Robert Jakob Alexander, died many years earlier in 1896, in a much less conventional way. I remember wondering where that grandfather had died, what might have happened to him, or where he was living when he died, but no one, not even my mother, seemed to know. By the time I was in high school I raised the question with our neighbor, Alfred Lang, a smooth-faced man of my parents' generation, who always wore too-wide blue-and-white-striped overalls, even in town, and lived with Allie, his mischievous wife on the adjoining farm just to the east. Unlike every other man with a farm to care for, Alfred had time to talk, and, in fact, you could often find him sitting in the kitchen even during daylight hours when the weather was good enough to work outdoors. For his neighbors, this was suspect, and for my father, even objectionable, behavior.

Alfred was filled with local information. After all, he'd lived in the same house all his life and loved to gossip, but you had to pry out the information a little bit at a time. The kitchen had an uneven wooden floor and a water bucket with a long-handled, enameled cup for drinking. The water was brought up from the cistern and tasted faintly of rust. From the window you looked across to a vegetable garden down by the Aermotor windmill and then up a long slope of pasture dotted with oaks and elms and hedge trees to the south. Like most farmers in this country before World War II, the Langs had a quarter section, 160 acres, of land. About half was farmed and the rest was native prairie, never broken to the plow.

Responding to my most recent query about the Alexander family, Alfred took up the subject. "Why, I'll tell you, those Alexander boys, Rein and Otto. They knew how to work. Lewis, too. Those boys built those farms."

That would be Reinhold, Otto, and Lewis Alexander, my mother's big, raw-boned older brothers, all dead fairly young; heart attacks, people said. The first two never married and lived alone on separate farms. They, too, died at home but not in the bosom of the family. Both had been dead on their farms for a number of days before they were found. Alfred, in fact, had found Otto, on his place a mile to the west, but I forget now who discovered Uncle Reinhold. He was found facedown on the concrete porch on the Alexander place—the homestead place—apparently trying to reach the screen door to the kitchen. I remember that my father, because of rain in the forecast, refused to stop baling hay so he and I never went to Uncle Reinhold's funeral. You can imagine my mother's reaction. Uncle Reinhold was a huge, jolly, simple man. When we heard the tick-clicking sound of his open Model T Ford swaying down the driveway, we knew we'd be in store for small sacks of jelly beans, a magnificent treat.

Alfred went through all these stories for me again. The fourth Alexander son was Robert, and Alfred knew a lot about him and so we reviewed his life as well. Uncle Robert had gone off in 1917 "to fight the Hun" (that is, to kill his distant cousins) on the Western front and survived despite being hit in the chest by machine gun bullets in the Meuse-Argonne campaign. On a later trip to our ancestral German village of Steinheim-an-der-Murr, I had been struck by how similar the names in the parish cemetery were to those in the Schaubel Cemetery. But there had been no doubt on whose side of World War I my father's sympathies lay; even German-speaking Grandpa Bauer supported the Allies and opposed the Kaiser.

Uncle Robert, in any case, survived and came back to another of the Alexander farms, this one only 80 acres, and a quiet and gentle life. During our visits to his and Aunt Ida's house, I would wait expectantly for him to lift me onto his knee and leaf patiently through the black-and-white photographs of a 3-inch-thick pictorial history of the war, which he did with a sweet smile, not apparently moved by pictures of the horrors he had undergone: all those tanks and trenches; barbed-wire; stark, shattered trees; mangled bodies. A bit later when my father, in a rare treat, took me to Clay Center to see the 1941 film *Sergeant York*, I was easily able to imagine Uncle Robert as the Gary Cooper character, an actor he actually strongly resembled.

But apart from his stories about the Alexander "boys," Alfred had occasionally brought up, or rather hinted, that there was something unusual about Grandfather Robert Alexander's death. A few years later, perhaps it was the summer I had come back on my first leave from the air force, I walked from our farm down to the Langs' place and was sitting in Alfred and Allie Lang's kitchen talking once more about my family history and mentioned Grandpa Alexander. Alfred mentioned, almost casually but with a certain reserve, "Your grandfather, you know, didn't die at home."

I wondered what that could mean but Alfred wouldn't say.

"You're too young to know that now," he said.

During one of my last visits to the Langs I walked again down the creek bank path, pressed down the bottom barbed wire with my foot, letting myself through the fence to visit Alfred and Allie. Their house remained pretty much the same even though Alfred had finally permitted the Rural Electrification Administration to string power lines through his wheat fields and bring electric lights to his house. But he still resisted replacing the Aermotor windmill with an electric pump, so the tin bucket and enameled cup I remembered from my earlier visits were still there.

He'd also, suddenly, become a lot older. He'd sold the farm and was soon to move to a tiny house in Green, last stop before the undertaker does his work. After instant coffee and store-bought cookies, I had to bring up again the question of my grandfather's mysterious death place.

This time he was prepared to talk.

"I think it was in the fall," he said. "Of course, I wasn't here, my dad told me the story. Do you really want to know?"

"Yes," I said.

"Well, that fall of 1896, Dad must have been sitting right where we are now. He told me he looked up to the south, across that prairie there, and saw a man leave your home place. It was late afternoon and cold; by the time he got about there"—Alfred pointed to a clump of hedge trees—"he was hunched over in the saddle like he was in lots of pain. . . . the Alexanders, they always had some good riding horses. We learned later that he had a burst appendix."

Alfred gummed one of the stale cookies. "Let's see now, where was I? Ah, you might have thought he was heading for town and a doctor.

But there was a woman living in the old Riechers place a mile east. Your grandfather left your grandmother and their eight kids that afternoon and went to that woman's house to die that night. That's why your grandfather didn't die at home."

13
Misbehavior

On Sundays, after family gatherings at Aunt Helen's, my sisters and our cousins and I would occasionally straggle along the country road a half-mile east and another half-mile north of Aunt Helen's and then, with a few backward glances and a little scared, we'd make our way down a long, unkempt driveway to an abandoned house. This was the "Bushell place." The doors weren't boarded over and we rather gingerly entered. Cousin Walter, Jr., at sixteen the oldest among us, whispered as we approached a back bedroom, "Here's where it happened." There was an unmade bed with scruffy moth-eaten blankets, signs of rats, floorboards raised up, and what young Walter said were blotches of dried blood on the walls.

What "had happened," more than ten years earlier on a winter night, Friday, December 23, 1930, was that a man called Bigler, carrying a baseball bat, had entered the bedroom of the house (and, apparently, the bed) that he shared with a hog trader named Baldwin, and crushed his partner's skull, spewing blood and brains against the plaster walls. The *Clay Center Times* reported the event in lurid—and touchingly ingenuous—prose. It turned out that the following Saturday, Warren Walquist, a young man living with his parents nearby, had been driving some cows along the road where a branch of Fancy Creek (just a mile upstream from our farm) flows in a culvert under the road, making a high bank on one side. One of the animals went off the bank down to the creek. Young Warren followed the cow and was surprised to find a Ford truck with a brightly painted red body and wheels and more alarming yet, the legs of a man protruding from under the truck. Warren ran home. His parents called Dr. MacIlvain, the coroner, and he and Sheriff Sparrowhawk came out to investigate. In the *Clay Center Times* story, the two men were puzzled by the scene, apparently unwilling to believe that a blatant murder had taken place on a peaceful country road.[1]

But at the same time, it required considerable imagination to believe that the bludgeoned man wrapped in a bloody bedsheet whose legs stuck out from under the truck had been driving the Ford or that the person or people who pushed the car over the bank had been dumb enough to place a dead man under the wheels. Consequently, Sparrowhawk soon "suspected that a killing had taken place." There were tracks in the snow of *two* cars and it was clear that part of the creek bank had been shoveled away, otherwise, the sheriff noticed, "the truck would not have gone over the bank." The coroner and Sheriff Sparrowhawk followed the car tracks back to the Bushell place. There they found bloody rags, an equally bloody baseball bat in the yard, and in the bedroom, a broken bed slat, and more blood on the walls, floor, and ceiling. They searched the barn and found bloody bedclothes and overalls. Sparrowhawk and the coroner "concluded that Baldwin had not died accidentally but had been killed"!

Bigler fled to a town just over the Nebraska border. Sheriff Sparrowhawk flew into action and found and arrested Bigler, who was tried, found guilty, and eventually sentenced to twenty years in prison. In a subsequent appeal he pled a case for self-defense and the sentence was reduced to two years.

A murder like the one that occurred on the Bushell place was not something that happened every day in Goshen Township, or even in Clay County. Out our way it was the only murder in the countryside anyone knew about—or at least talked about over many years. In fact, it's *still* talked about. On May 13, 2011, I interviewed two octogenarian cousins in Clay Center and in response to my query, both discussed the Bigler-Baldwin case in remarkable detail, remembering the names of the two principals, the make and color of the Ford truck, the bloodstained bedclothes, and the flight to Nebraska. An apparently all-inclusive "Homicide Folder" in the Clay Center Museum contains only thirty-six cases between 1877 and 2005, almost all occurring in recent years. Small wonder that the Bigler-Baldwin murder, eighty-one years later, remains in the collective memory.

Generally speaking, we lived an unnoticed, peaceful life. No doubt things went on that were *not* talked about. But no one on the farms locked the farmhouse or barn door; I can't remember, except for the keys in cars, even seeing or turning a key. We never had anything stolen but sometimes a lent tool or rake or shovel might, through neglect, be returned late and we had to go track it down. There's a newspaper account that someone robbed the Green Post Office twice between 1922 and 1935; we wanted to believe that the Dalton gang tried to rob a bank in Clay Center, and bootleggers were occasionally seen on the back roads, but rarely apprehended. We heard the account of benign small-town events in the case of one Thetus Lewis, who on June 1, 1949, was charged with being drunk in a public place. A constable fined him $5 plus court costs of $12.29, "both of which he paid and was released."[2]

You rarely heard of *physical* domestic violence—either interspousal or regarding children—in part, I suppose, because as always, such things are usually not reported, or because there's no one to report them to. Then too, one might speculate that since both husband and wife (and children) were indispensable to the economic success of the farm, this fact *may* have led to less domestic violence, to a more cooperative familial union. It's impossible to know. Shame and scorn would have attached to any man beating his wife, and although the Clay Center papers reported the fairly small number of homicides, domestic violence only in the rarest cases made the press. Then, too, to whom would such transgressions have been reported? The only peacekeeping agents in the entire county consisted of a sheriff and his deputy in Clay Center, and someone called a "constable" in the small towns. Growing up, I never saw or heard of such a person.

Like everyone else on the planet, our neighbors, aunts, uncles, and cousins had their secret longings and desires, even in this unsexualized society. On a moonless summer night, I think in 1941, Uncle Paul, returning from town with Grandma Nettie in his 1936 Chevrolet, came over a rise on one of the dirt roads 3 miles down from our farm and bumped into the rear of a parked car. The surprised driver sped off into the night. During the subsequent few days—the event was too scandalous to keep quiet—there was lots of murmured speculation that reached even my ten-year-old ears. It occurred to Uncle Paul, consumed with curiosity in the midst of the gossip, to return to the scene of the crime, where he found in the weeds pieces of a broken rear reflector.

A few days later he took the shards to several automobile repair shops in Clay Center and found that the broken pieces matched those of a car identical to that of a handsome middle-aged man who lived some miles away on the road to Green. Rumors soon spread that he had been parked there with another man's woman (why else would he have parked there?). The event was talked about for several years—again, like the Bigler-Baldwin case, it's *still* remembered down to the year and model of the car. I don't believe the gentleman ever lived down his reputation. If the woman were known, her name, as far as I know, was not mentioned.

A rare case of untoward behavior involved the farm family adjoining our place on the north. The George Riek family consisted of George, the taciturn patriarch; his wife; son Harold and wife; a daughter, Mae; and a young boy, two years younger than I, called Donnie Bolin. Three other daughters, all named for flowers—Lily, Violet, and Rose—were married and lived on farms in other townships.

My cousins and I couldn't help but wonder how Donnie Bolin fit into the Riek family. Did he have a dad and where was he? Or a mother? Was "Aunt Mae," who lived in the Riek family, really his mother, as some gossip had it? After a bit, there was hearsay that his real mother, called Lenora, worked in a restaurant in Manhattan but she seemed never to come visit. Our parents and neighbors maintained the most hermetic silence on the subject, simply ignoring our question or repeating that of course he had a mother who worked in another town and Aunt Mae was taking care of Donnie until he grew up.

Donnie Bolin was, of course, the result of the regular calls of a "traveling salesman" on the "farmer's daughter." Donnie's mysterious background complicated our notion of family and mothers and dads. After two or three years, Imogene Stetnisch, the bold, thirteen-year-old daughter of the farmhand who lived across the road, explained the situation for us, mincing neither words nor graphic detail.

And people lived lives of quiet desperation. Betty Hofmann, the blacksmith's wife, and mother of Donnie Hofmann, was brought up in a fairly large town many miles away. My mother and Betty were close friends but many other farm wives cocked a skeptical eye at her city ways. Some time after I left the farm and Donnie went to California, she sat down in her spotless kitchen, pulled a small .22-caliber revolver from her purse, and killed herself with a single shot to the head.

14
Church

My great-grandfather, Johann Jakob Bauer, and his wife, Katharina, like many other German immigrants of their time and place, came to America with their young family as life-loving Lutherans. They planted cuttings of the vine, made wine; my parents even talked of barn dances when they were young. A long generation or so later, however, in the struggle to sustain settlement in Goshen Township, Kansas, their three surviving sons and a daughter seem to have lost not only their old-world piety but also their exuberance for ordinary pleasures. Many drifted away from the Lutheran church into a kind of religious apathy. At the same time, several families and individuals in our neighborhood—including most definitely my grandma Bauer—fell victim to the appeal of severe Protestant churches. For them, playing cards became the Devil's pasteboards, vines were uprooted, corners of mouths turned firmly down. Many of the families of these cheerless sects lived—as H. L. Mencken put it in the well-known line about Puritanism—with the haunting fear that somewhere, someone may be happy.

There were several different religions of European origin that accompanied the mosaic of settlement in Kansas. We might even begin with the Franciscan friar Juan de Padilla—the first clergyman, Catholic or Protestant, in Kansas—who accompanied Vásquez de Coronado's intrusion in 1541. He worked among the Wichita tribes that year and returned to gain his martyrdom the following year. French Jesuits—the famous "black robes"—entered Kansas in 1724; other Catholic missions carried out the first baptism of the Osage in 1822; Methodists, Quakers, Presbyterians, and Dunkards followed in the 1830s. A large migration of Mennonites appeared in south-central Kansas in the 1870s while Lutherans became dominant in the northern plains.

The two most established congregations in our part of Kansas were the Swedish Lutherans and Irish Catholics. Both built imposing, flourishing churches filled with parishioners. The Catholics were suspected of not being proper Americans, but instead, of taking their orders from Rome—a notion that persisted during John F. Kennedy's campaign for the presidency. The Lutheran church was 7 miles west of our farm; the Catholics, just to the north.[1]

By the 1880s, farms and farmers in our own specific community were sufficiently thick on the ground to make up the critical mass needed to erect a building for the United Brethren Church, a solid, modest, dun-colored edifice 2 miles north of our farm, the nearest temple of the spiritual life. This building also offered religious shelter to small, nearby groups of Congregationalists and Dunkards. On Sundays we'd see five or six Dunkard women, plainly dressed in long dresses and black and white bonnets, slowly making their way on foot past our driveway toward the UBC.

With their church built out of local limestone and finished in 1890–1891 (and wired for electricity in the early 1940s by my father), local United Brethrens joined hands with congregations in the nearby towns of Green and Leonardville to hire a series of itinerant ministers. The local United Brethrens merged to form the Evangelical United Methodists in 1946.

On summer Sunday mornings, across from the church, there were usually a few men accustomed to gathering alongside the blacksmith shop to pitch horseshoes, and during church services one could hear the clang of shoes hitting the stake. On one occasion at least, this led the pious to complain to the circuit preacher. Apparently unflappable, he pointed out that he'd prefer to have the men pitch horseshoes and think of God than sit in his church thinking about horseshoes.

Although not everyone was an ardent believer, almost everyone in our neighborhood went to church on Sunday morning. Two front rows off the aisle were reserved for a sturdy men's choir in which Uncle Walter's voice was notable as it belted out familiar hymns. After service—if the weather was good—everyone gathered outside, exchanging news, talking with the preacher. The congregation also sponsored church plays at Easter and Christmas; church socials that provided other opportunities for getting together with the neighbors; and of course, a site for marriages and funeral services. The church was one more institution in our landscape that contributed to a sense of community, even if my own family was marginal to it.

My grandmother Bauer, originally from a German Lutheran background, chose the United Brethren Church at Fact because of geography: the proper Lutheran church was 7 miles away. Grandma Nettie was a grim and faithful member of the church. On Sundays she'd drive up from the home place to our farm, dropping Grandpa William Jakob off at the house where he dandled us on his knee—my sister Irene was his favorite—taking joyous drags on the Niles Moser cigar forbidden at home, while Grandma continued on another mile to church. But very rarely did anyone else in our family join Grandma Nettie in the open Buick roadster to drive to Sunday services. Our family stayed together even if we didn't pray together.

Grandma Nettie liked to talk to me about the Bible and particularly about the moment of her acceptance of Jesus as her personal savior. That occurred one day after she had been playing a hymn on the piano at the home place and we were sitting at the kitchen table. "I felt my spirit rise up," she said, lifting her arms heavenward, "all my cares disappeared, and they've never returned." I, of course, at preadolescence, was foreign to such sentiments although usually respectful at the table. Grandma offered buttered and sugar-sprinkled slices of a freshly baked loaf. With both eyes closed and downcast, she pronounced the simple prayer,

> "Bless this food to our use and us to thy service
> For the sake of thy son Jesus Christ, amen."

I remember, to my shame, brattishly peeking to see if Grandmother's eyes remained tightly closed while saying grace.

⟫⟫•⟪⟪

Just why, in the local landscape of believers and churchgoers, most members of both my paternal and maternal families—the Bauers and the Alexanders—did not take a more active interest in our local

United Brethren Church—or in religion in general—is hard to determine, and particularly so in a world where written records are scant and few reveal sentimental or spiritual values. I've not found memoirs or accounts of church attendance, or anything that might reveal how my family thought or felt about religion. There are copies of a handful of letters written to relatives left behind in Germany that tell of crop failure, of good soil for apple and peach trees, and of the difficulty of digging for good water. The letters mention children and give accounts of births and deaths, but the inner life remains, as one might expect, obscured. I noticed, for example, that my mother's civil documents—birth certificate, marriage license, school records—were of course in English; her 1896 Lutheran baptism scroll, however, is in German, suggesting the persistence of the original religious culture. But evidence of religious *feeling* is hard to come by. My mother's father and at least one uncle studied for the Lutheran ministry, in Germany, but little of the religiosity—in the case of this family—seems to have carried over to the Kansas plains.

One afternoon, home on a weekend during my first year at Kansas State, I found on a neglected shelf over the stairway the large, ornate, hardcover Bible of the Alexander family. Sitting at the dining room table with my mother, I was moved to try to explain something about the nature of that book, beginning with the story of Genesis and the ancient Hebrews, skipping forward to the stories about Jesus. I must have made it all sound tremendously unreal. "That's all too much for me," she said. "I just can't take that in."

It *is* peculiar that my particular family had so little interest in church or religion. I doubt that I attended church service more than five times in an entire year. I did perform in the Easter and Christmas performances, although in minor roles. On one occasion I played the part of one of the Magi. My sisters and I were not encouraged to attend church and were given no formal religious instruction or, for that matter, even baptized, as both my parents had been. The only time I can remember my father actually present in church—and the only time I ever saw a tear fall from his eye—was at his own father's funeral. We were a family given to neither spiritual nor emotional excess.

The explanation for our particular family's alienation from church surely rests not so much on my father's opposition to church or religion but rather his indifference to the entire subject. For him, the spiritual life occupied another sphere, out there in a different and unknowable universe; there were so many things to do and so little time in this life. He drove very fast, trailing streams of dust along the road, and the neighbors learned to be on the lookout, pulling over to the side to let his pickup, and much later his huge, black, tail-finned Cadillac, roar by. There were houses and outbuildings to wire, machinery to repair, that new coal-burning furnace to put in the basement. And reading—"I never get a chance to read," he'd complain—not to mention work on the farm, fixing fence, raising the new Hereford steers he'd bought at a sale, and a thousand other things that came up. Other men who did go to church were not exactly idle, but my father, above all, was a doer, always busy, even driven. There's no obvious explanation for that, either—it's the way he was. No doubt those anticlerical notions seeped into my and my sisters' brains. Irene, too, thought the whole business of church and religion a waste of time.

Anyway, we—and, very rarely, my father—did go to Christmas service at the United Brethren Church. The best part of Christmas Eve, however, was going directly across the gravel road in the blowing snow to the warm comfort of the gruff blacksmith's house, racing around the kitchen with Donnie Hofmann, and sampling the pies, cakes, and cookies laid out by Mrs. Hofmann.

15
School

When Kansas was admitted to the Union in 1861, the federal government required that the state set aside two square-mile sections (of 640 acres) in each township, the sale or rental of which would generate revenue for the establishment and support of public schools. In the entire state this amounted to nearly 3 million acres. In 1864, the state legislature approved the sale of these school lands with the proviso that the sales themselves be delayed three years in order to take advantage of rising land prices. The going price in the years 1867–1882 was around $3 to $4 an acre.[1] The salutary effect of the school lands policy was felt almost immediately, where in Goshen Township alone, *five* one-room rural schools—Diamond, Schaubel, Idylwild, Pleasant Valley, and Fairfield—sprung into existence between 1866 and 1870. They served the primary educational needs of the approximately 140 farm families that in 1880 comprised a total population of 965 in the 36-square-mile township, a typically dense settlement pattern for this part of Kansas. Five schools in such a small space ensured that few children had to walk more than 2 or 3 miles to school.

My own school, Fairfield School District #24, opened in 1870, a mile and a half north of our farm, a half-mile south of Fact. The school, set on a square acre, was a one-room, wood-frame building with a small coat closet at the entrance and a raised stage at the far end. The entrance faced south to avoid the blasts of snow, which in this country come sifting in from the north. At the far corners of the square acre were outhouses for boys and girls; next to the school stood a small, rude, iron merry-go-round, a simple teeter-totter, a single swing; and near this, a coal house where my father stored a few bales of hay for the days I rode my pony to school. There was a thicket of

Fairfield School District #24. Teacher Wandalea Kimbrough is on upper right; I'm standing, center row third from the right; Donnie Hofmann is on my right.

dogwood alongside the coalhouse and a scraggly lilac by the cistern. Inside, perhaps twenty-four desks, all the same size, were aligned in four, or maybe five, rows facing the stage, each with a built-in inkwell and the initials of past students carved into the varnished desktop. A large, black, potbellied wood- or coal-burning stove, hard for the teacher to start in the winter mornings, gave out adequate heat.

Nostalgia for the dying, and now mostly dead, one-room rural school has become something of a cliché in the past few years as older people fondly romanticize a down-home, decidedly unglamorous, bare-bones institution. In a larger sense, its formal establishment in Kansas in the 1860s and 70s was a valuable instrument in the creation of a literate, English-speaking, educated citizenry out of a flood of polyglot immigrants in the course of the nineteenth and twentieth centuries. Along with the various Homestead Acts, the rural school policy provides a fundamental explanation for the very different paths to democracy and economic progress among the new republics of the Western Hemisphere. In 1920 there were still nearly 200,000 rural one-room schools; today (2011) there are fewer than 200.

Our teacher, my first four years, was Wandalea—pronounced "Wanda Lee"—Kimbrough, daughter of Cass and Blanche, who in appearance took after her plump mother. Wandalea was a competent, affectionate person. She was not just the sole teacher for the full eight grades; she was also—like all other teachers—principal, advisor, and disciplinarian. She sat at her desk on the raised stage facing us, frequently glancing into a small round mirror to pinch her pimples and fluff up her hair in order to be prepared, it seemed, for an unannounced visit from her boyfriend and future husband, stationed nearby in Fort Riley.

Mr. Victor Hedlund, fresh out of high school Normal Training, replaced Wandalea. Mr. Hedlund, we all observed, wore the same pair of brown wool trousers with a dime-sized hole in the leg the entire term. Occasionally, Mr. Hedlund was driven mad by the swirling multiple tasks and the frustration of dealing with eight grades in a single room at the same time. A full twenty years old, thus nearly the same age as the two lanky boys in the back row whose progress through primary school was delayed by farmwork, Mr. Hedlund, now and then apparently exasperated beyond measure, stalked down the aisle and gave some kids, such as the independent-minded Imogene Stetnisch, terrific slaps across the back with his open hand. Once, aiming too low, his fingers caught the 3-inch wooden rise on the desk, causing Mr. Hedlund to wring his hand in pain, leaving Imogene defiant but provoking nearly uncontrollable snickers in everyone else. He lasted one year.

Next was the very jolly Mary Lee Hanson, likewise a recent high school graduate. Mary Lee often boarded at our house during the winter. Since she was my sister's good high school pal, and because my father was head of the school board, we charged her nothing for the overnight stays. I remember the laughter, the card games, the Chinese checkers that even my father joined in. Then, the following morning at first light—if the trapping season was over—joined by Donnie Bolin and the Dankenbring twins who fell in along the way, we'd all— teacher and kids—walk together to school, sometimes with the air so still that snow was piled up on the tree branches, and bunny rabbits—

"cottontails"—huddled down in their hedgerow nests, so stiff from cold they didn't budge, unblinkingly watched us go by.

Finally, the last teacher, in my eighth year, was the severe Mrs. Sparman, who wore her grey hair in a tightly wound bun and was determined to teach us all to play the harmonica. To our barely restrained giggles, she indicated the directions as "this-a-way" and "that-a-way," and pronounced the word "Sioux," for the Indians who had done in General Custer, as "Sigh-ox." Just why the kids, who probably never heard the word aloud, knew how it was properly pronounced while the teacher didn't is curious.

⇒◦⇐

I don't want to give a false impression of the underpaid, heroic teachers of rural schools. A great many of these one-room schoolteachers who accompanied the settlement of Kansas were highly competent, intelligent, selfless, dedicated, and experienced people. Although it's true that Fairfield School District #24 did have a mixed bag of teachers, somehow, in the midst of all this, we managed to learn basic arithmetic, penmanship, geography (helped along, as I've mentioned, by the war news), and—although not in my case—to play the piano or harmonica. I have the impression that we read a lot and we certainly did at home where my father subscribed to several magazines and bought books whenever he could. I must say, immodestly, that I was the top student in my class of five and actually the teacher's favorite all through the eight grades. Both my mother and father highly praised their own teachers in the Schaubel School, and indeed, my father in his eight years of study learned to write an expressive, even elegant, English.

One-room rural schoolteachers were often single and female—in fact, the contracts often required this. In the case of Fairfield School District #24, none of our teachers had trained beyond the high school diploma in Normal Training and they earned $65 a month for nine months. If the "schoolmarm" (or "school dad") did not live within easy reach of the school, she might—like Mary Lee—board with one of the farm families in the district when snow blocked the roads.

Despite the isolated landscape and unglamorous routine of most rural teachers, now and then—rarely—a prospective beau might appear at the schoolhouse door. The story of Uncle Frank, one of our more exotic ancestors—indeed, perhaps the only one—illustrates the improbable side of at least one of the local schoolmarms' lives. In his youth, Uncle Frank was tall, slender, and handsome, with unruly hair and a wide, black moustache. Rather than the common farmer uniform of loose, blue-and-white-striped overalls held in place by galluses and usually unbuttoned at the sides, Uncle Frank wore tweed trousers, a denim shirt, and a kind of Australian outback hat pitched at a jaunty angle (unlike the army officer's cap in the picture on page 94). Thinking back to those innocent days, he seemed to me—although I didn't know then the words—a bit devilish, a rogue. In a different age, in another setting, he would have been a dandy, a *galan*. He was my mother's favorite uncle.

When Uncle Frank was around thirty, at the turn of the twentieth century, he fell in love with the young, pretty teacher of the Schaubel School, one Beatrice Lathrop. They spent what must have been the most exotic honeymoon imaginable, taking the train to St. Louis at the time of the 1904 World's Fair. Alas, there is a melancholy end: two years later Beatrice died in childbirth.

———◦———

In our school, the teacher was responsible not only for some eighteen students distributed through all eight grades but also for developing and staging the Parent/Teacher Association meetings three or four evenings of the year. These were enthusiastically attended by the local families, who brought sandwiches and cakes for evening refreshments and provided entertainment as well. This was often in the form of grown-up tap dancers, banjo or fiddle players, or singers from the surrounding farms—lots of local talent. The students usually presented skits or readings. I made my debut in the first grade. I walked unsteadily up the left aisle to the stage, turned right, faced the enormous, terrifying crowd, and recited from memory the following verse, which I want to think brought down the house:

"I had a little awl,
Stuck it in the wall,
That's all."

———◆———

Another feature of the Parent/Teacher Association's evening meetings was the box social, a cultural institution widely practiced across the United States, in our case to raise money for the school. Girls and unmarried women in the district went to considerable lengths not only to prepare an elaborate meal—usually some combination of cold meat, canned bean salad, cookies, and slices of pie or cake—but also to present the food in a gaily wrapped box or basket. After the business at hand ended, each box or basket was auctioned off; the man making the winning bid was then permitted to sit and dine with the young woman who had prepared the boxed supper. The young—and some not so young—women tried to disguise their work to prevent unwanted purchase by an unsuitable man, while at the same time subtly tipping their identity to a more eligible beau. But because of audible speculation, the men were usually able to scout out the creator's identity by poking about among the various offerings displayed on long tables before the auction began. Once the fun began, there was spirited and good-humored bidding. This occasionally led to unanticipated dining partners and even to serious but unacknowledged disappointment. I remember particularly the persistence of Homer Sanneman in outbidding rivals for cousin Wilene's company.

You could always count on Homer's participation at these gatherings, in part because he knew Wilene would be present, but also because he made reliable contributions to the entertainment hour, belting out—usually to Wilene's accompaniment on the piano—his preferred song (and a favorite among the guests):

"Brighten the corner where you are
Brighten the corner where you are
Someone far from harbor
You may guide across the bar."

Uncle Frank Riechers alongside his 1908 Buick.

My class of five, including Donnie Hofmann, the Dankenbring twins, and Mary Siebold, was the largest single cohort during my eight years in Fairfield District. We moved in lockstep through the grades, since usually no one moved in or out of the community. Imogene Stetnisch, daughter of a day laborer, was the only exception, entering into the class ahead of me in midterm. She was, indeed, the only addition to the school except, of course, for the new crop of first graders each year. A couple of big, galumphing farm kids of seventeen or eighteen, who were able to attend school for only a few months of the year because of duties on their farms, squeezed into the desks at the back.

The older kids had an obvious advantage in the annual Field Day competition of high and broad jumps, relay races, sack races, and a variety of other games. They were held in the town of Green, some 8 or 9 miles away, and chosen in part because they required no expensive equipment or even special shoes. We were awarded blue, red, and white ribbons, proudly displayed at home.

In my seventh or eighth year of school on a warm spring evening—I'd like to think the dogwood was in bloom—while our parents were holding one of the Parent/Teacher meetings inside the schoolroom, several of us students were darting around outside the school, playing tag or perhaps hide-and-seek. Whether flowers were out or not, I certainly do remember that first exquisite sense of soft female flesh—the onset of the tyranny of sex—here in the form of thirteen-year-old Joan, the prettier of the Dankenbring twins. Maybe we bumped or touched while playing; perhaps, more advanced, she teased me. Impulsively, I lifted Joan and whirled her about in my arms; the scent of that girl, of that warm body, came through the summer dress. There were open-mouthed ohs and ahs from the other kids, and for the next several weeks and maybe even months, the other kids remembered that night as "the time Arnold picked up Joan Dankenbring." Obviously, I remember it, too.

Fairfield School District #24 was abandoned and burned twenty years ago. All that remains is the cracked cover of the old cistern and the concrete footings.

16
Depression and Drought

The prosperity of the late 1920s actually carried over into the Depression and drought years longer than people believe. On March 15, 1934, while the early policies of the New Deal were faltering, the 160-acre Kulp farm adjoining ours to the south sold for an impressive $40 an acre for a total of $6,400. As late as 1935, with the dust storms already upon us, a neighbor's wheat made thirty bushels to the acre.[1] But then, our farm and, for that matter, all of the surrounding country were hit by the twin onslaughts of the Great Depression and a devastating drought. My early years in Fairfield School District #24 coincided with hard times for our farm, and on several days we were sent home from school at noon, the sun barely visible in the blowing dust.

A great depression is something that today would send many folks off to the therapist, but for us it meant the collapse of the first big cycle of liberal capitalism that lasted from about the 1870s down to 1930. No one described it like that, of course, and I imagine that most ordinary people had little understanding of what was happening. In New York and other big cities we heard (turned out not to be true) that stockbrokers were jumping out of the windows of skyscrapers and there were newspaper pictures of long lines of people out of work all across the United States. Some of these people were put to work building roads and bridges, and we saw groups of men in a kind of work-clothes uniform standing along the road, having been hauled out from somewhere in trucks. The Works Progress Administration (WPA), one of President Roosevelt's New Deal agencies, aimed at giving some of the millions of unemployed a job, hired these men.

Most of the farmers where we lived didn't like the idea of the government handing out jobs, especially when they saw these men standing around, leaning on their shovels. They scornfully joked that WPA must stand for "We Putter Around." Now and then we saw hobos (migrant workers) come along the road from the south, apparently off the railroad from Clay Center, looking for work. They were not welcome and were seen as faintly threatening. My mother would shoo me back into the kitchen, stand in the half-opened door drying her palms on her apron, and explain that we had no work, no jobs for them. This disappointing but hardly surprising dismissal was occasionally accompanied by a slice of freshly baked bread. During these same years we'd occasionally hear the tinkle of bells, the clip-clop of mules, and strange cries, as gypsies, the men plain, the women wrapped in flowing exotic dresses and scarves, came down the road in their flimsy covered wagons offering to sharpen knives or to sell trinkets and lengths of cloth that we wouldn't have been caught dead in. The gypsies, like the hobos, were suspect, and to us rather more ominous.

The Great Depression meant lower and lower prices for the things we produced. Wheat, our main crop, dropped from $2.50 a bushel in the late 1920s to under 50 cents six years later. At one point, the order came out from Washington that farmers were to slaughter their hogs to drive up prices. This simply seemed wrong—and was more than my father could bear—and he never voted for Roosevelt again (he had in 1932), even though he admired the great Tennessee Valley Authority project of dams and electricity generators and of course, a bit later, the REA that brought electric power to the farms.

Another New Deal program provided 1-gallon tins of food, with a plain white adhesive label, for the really poor people. There was only one family in my school district, the Siebolds, that qualified for—or would accept—the program. The Siebold family included twelve children, four of whom were in one or another of the eight grades in Fairfield School District #24. They brought the welfare tins to school for lunch, and although I wasn't sure just what the "food" was—I remember a kind of powdered substance to mix with water—I would have been happy to trade a cup of it for one of the cold pork chops wrapped in oilpaper that mother sent along for my lunch. When I got home from school and reported on the Siebolds' tinned food, my father made it *very* clear that we were *never to touch*, under any circumstances, those "government hand-outs."

Owning our own farm, having no mortgage, and being basically self-sufficient, we were better able to ride out the lean times. We had milk and eggs and enough wheat to exchange for flour, and, except in the worst of times, our garden provided fresh vegetables for the table and the surplus to can.

———————

If, however, the Depression was bearable, the second onslaught of the 1930s was more difficult. For five or six years during that decade, the rain stopped falling. And so, like never before in the local people's memory, an unrelenting drought settled over a wide swath of the Midwest, including our part of Kansas. Crops dried up, animals died of thirst, and soon the winds whipped up the dry, plowed soil into towering dust storms. The dust entered through every crack so that you could write your name in dust on the round oak dining room table only a few minutes after mother had "dusted." She put dishtowels in the doorjambs but still the dust filtered through.

Adding to our misery, in the depths of the drought, on July 16, 1936—the year and day were engraved in local people's memory—the leading edge of a dense cloud of grasshoppers swept through the country. In three days of voracious assault, they devoured whatever green leaf or sprig they could find, defoliating trees, forming a crust on the stock tanks. There were exaggerated tales of their blotting out the sun and eating the wooden pitchfork handles. One neighbor claimed that they ate the paint off the north side of his house. Their bodies crashed into the window screen or, if you ventured outside, into your hair and face, their mouths emitting a repellent brown liquid that someone called "tobacco juice."

In desperation my father found half a truckload of watermelons, perhaps already overripe or spoiled. We broke them open, sloshed poison into their red watery flesh, and scattered them around the fields hoping somehow that the grasshoppers would prefer them to green plants. They didn't.

All of this seems now like a disaster of biblical proportions, which indeed it was. Some farmers were unable to pay their mortgages and lost their farms to the bank, but most of the people I knew, and certainly our relatives, managed to survive. The creeks ran dry but the well held out; somehow, we kept the horses and cattle alive. Grandmother Alexander kept her farm and her sons kept theirs, and Grandfather William Bauer held on to the 320-acre home place and the four other farms assigned to his sons. Elsewhere in the Dust Bowl, thousands of people bailed out to towns and, so to speak, greener pastures. Farther south, on the poorer lands of Oklahoma and northern Texas, the drought, combined with falling prices, drove people west to California, to endure the grapes of wrath.

<hr />

My father's survival strategy was to build a sawmill. He drew up the plans on the dining room table lit by a kerosene, or maybe a Coleman, lamp; graded the site with a team of mules; salvaged long 12 x 12-inch creosoted beams from a dismantled railway bridge for the frame; and had the blacksmith help him weld together the movable carriage on which the logs moved into a circular saw, purchased from St. Louis. An ancient steam engine tractor, complete with bells and whistles and fired with scraps of dry lumber, provided power. The sawmill was originally set up in an uncultivated grove of cottonwood trees across the road from our farm, and neighboring farmers brought, in horse-hauled wagons, their own logs, mostly cottonwood, with some cedar and oak and black walnut, to be cut into planks and boards. I made the cedar chest in the bedroom and the walnut bed in my study in the house where I now live in a high school manual training course from trees sawed by my father in his mill. I also crafted a pair of small end tables, presently alongside my daughter's sofa in Brooklyn. Dare I hope that these rustic heirlooms will not disappear?

When the local source of trees became exhausted, my father dismantled the mill, loaded it up on several squealing steel-wheeled wagons, hitched them to the steam tractor, and moved the entire contraption at a barely discernable pace of 4 miles per hour to Morganville, 15 miles west on the Republican River, where trees were more abundant. There, F. W. and his crew of four or five men set up the mill again, worked from dawn to dusk, and stayed over in two- or three-week shifts in the wheeled dorm and "cook shack" that accompanied the train of wagons towed by the steam engine. Meanwhile, back on the farm, my mother took over the chores, gardened, cooked and cleaned, sold a smaller amount of eggs and cream than previously, and we pressed on with our lives.

I've gone on a bit about the sawmill because it created quite a sensation around the country, and my father was judged very clever for designing and building an entire sawmill and fixing up the old steam engine. And, although my father was reluctant to charge an adequate price for his work, the mill must have helped him ride out the Depression and drought.

Unlike the situation of the army of unemployed or half-employed workers that one glimpsed in the towns or on the roads, the family farm provided a shield against really dire circumstances. Maybe because I was a kid, I was insulated from family tensions and anxieties. Yet when a question arose about whether one of my sisters should be allowed to buy some small item (I forget what), I complained, explaining that "we can't buy that, we're poor." My mother was amused. I don't believe that she or any of my family thought of ourselves as "poor"; I don't recall anyone feeling envy or resentment toward better-off families, although my mother did inveigh against some of the pretentiousness of city folk—that is, people from Clay Center.

Late in his life, I asked my father what the worst years of his life were. "Why, the thirties," he said. "You don't know anything about that; the drought, the Depression, those were hard times."

"And the best times?" I asked, a day or so later. He thought for a few minutes. "The thirties, I think, when you children were at home and we all worked together."

It's also true that the Depression had an enduring effect on me that continues to the present. I can't bear to throw things away, particularly food. I eat the blackened bananas first (which means I hardly ever enjoy a fresh yellow one); when the shampoo or dish soap runs out, I swish water into the empty flask; in the stick-shift days, I'd coast downhill to save gas; I have frazzled shirt collars turned; can't bear to see abandoned, half-empty Coke cans lying about in the house. In fact, I can hardly bear to see any soft-drink cans half empty *or* full.

17
Having Company

As we emerged from the Depression and drought in the late thirties and early forties and bought more reliable cars, we engaged a bit more in the custom of "going visiting." My grandparents' generation produced lots of children: seven in the Bauer family, eight in the Alexander. That added up to lots of uncles and aunts for me (even though they were not always on speaking terms) and lots of cousins, not to mention the nonrelatives we knew on adjoining farms. Most other families were large and generally chose their mates locally, so people were thick on the ground, and since we knew almost all of them, there were many places to "go visiting," and, in turn, we received lots of "company."

The aim of my grandfather William Bauer, like many of his generation, had been to acquire through hard work on the original settlement enough money to purchase quarter-section farms for each of the sons. One hundred and sixty acres, properly worked, provided a decent living for a family. The daughters were expected, as many did—as my mother did—to marry the sons of other farmers. This was less true of my generation. Quite a few of my female cousins married local men but my own sisters would never have considered it.

Why, I do not know. Disdain for our fellow farmers? An uncharacteristic and unfortunate notion of superiority? Did they sense an unexpressed disappointment in our father's life at not having been able to participate in a larger world, and they themselves vowed to leave the farm? Did they see our father, with his books and magazines and mechanical talent, as a cut above our neighbors' level, and consequently thought that they, too, deserved better? Such attitudes were certainly not in accord with my mother's praise for people who were as common as an old shoe. Whatever the reason, my sisters left after high school and didn't look back.

⟞⬧⟝

In any case, my parents and I had lots of people to visit. The distractions of movies, or other urban vices, were still 15 miles away; consequently, we had few things other than "visiting" to do for entertainment. There were additional reasons. There was often a sense of connection, of shared interests and shared problems that could be discussed and resolved with our neighbors' help. We exchanged machinery and tools, lent our team of workhorses, helped find and catch stray animals, and even found local remedies for unbearable toothaches. I overheard one day an urgent telephone conversation between my father and our neighbor George Riek. Dad slammed the phone down on the hook, pulled out from behind the cupboard a hidden halfbottle of whisky that we had no idea was there, poured himself a stiff shot, and roared off in the Olds to Mr. Riek, who yanked out the offending molar with his pliers.

Much later, forty years after we'd both left the farm, my sister and I sketched out on her breakfast table in Tucson, where she had retired, a free-hand map of the 36 square miles of Goshen Township. We were still able to remember at least half of all the farm families and the names of all of our closer neighbors who had lived there when we were growing up. We were, in that now usually ill-used term, a community.

So we "went visiting" quite a lot. If summer rain kept us out of the fields, or if the early darkness of spring or late autumn provided an opportunity in the evenings, we went calling on nearby farms, and in turn, neighbors and relatives came to us. This was called "having company." These visits occasionally caught the attention of the "local news" columns of the Clay Center newspapers, such as "Mr. and Mrs. Kenneth Lloyd visited at the Ramer Sanneman family on Thursday."[1]

As soon as supper was over and the dishes washed up, you looked for headlights in the long driveway, hoping it was someone you liked. I used to hope the visitors were my favorites, Aunt Helen and Uncle

Walter, or Uncle Gerald and Aunt Irene. Alfred and Allie Lang, Betty and Clarence Hoffman, Charley and Ruth Riechers, and even cousin John Bauer and wife Mae from as far away as Morganville were, along with many others, frequent company. Their children usually came along and we'd have a good time scattering to the fields to catch lightning bugs or playing hide-and-seek among the buildings, or simply lying down, looking at the stars, a little nervous in the broad night.

As a rule, no one called up on the party line before visiting; a car just appeared; but wherever you went, or when visitors came to us, the woman of the house always seemed to have a pie or cake or cookies tucked away in the pantry that were brought out with coffee for the grown-ups. At that point, the men came in off the porch, sat about rather awkwardly, dropped their talk of plowing or prices, and remained silent while the women continued their discussion of canning, or about so-and-so's (mildly) scandalous behavior.

At other times, a number of housewives would get together to organize larger gatherings for a kind of "pitch party"—pitch being the favorite card game—in one of the neighborhood farmhouses, frequently ours. After the game, there was occasionally a special treat. The women would go into the kitchen and heat up a white, thin, milky oyster stew; stir up the whole, slimy, grey-black oysters from the bottom of the pot; and ladle out portions to the adults. The stew came in gallon-sized tins marked with a crudely typed, maybe even handwritten, label. During the previous week, the highly anticipated oyster stew was the subject of telephone discussion on the party line. I have no sense of where such a dish was acquired. Not locally—oysters were certainly not common in Clay County. Was it brought back in a cattle truck returning from Kansas City? Could it have been one of Franklin Roosevelt's New Deal handouts? Let's hope not. Anyway, oyster stew was exotic, reserved entirely for grown-ups. Most of us kids thought it disgusting.

Aunt Helen and Uncle Walter were my favorites to *go to* visit. She was a stout, full-breasted, powerful woman with a broad brow and severely pulled-back hair. Her reading glasses magnified large brown eyes. Religious out of convention, if not conviction, and more than a little self-righteous, she often emitted cluck-clucking admonitions about the improper behavior of other families. But at the same time, she was a large, warm presence. She took you in, engaged you, asked about your little friends like Donnie Hoffman, about war stories in the *Topeka Daily Capitol*, and, later, even about girls that I'd met in high school, something the men, of course, never did, except to tease. Aunt Helen was my mother's good friend and a good bridge between the Bauer and Alexander families.

Uncle Walter, tall, slim, nervous, arms waving wildly, would come out and stand in the yard to greet us as we drove our car into the driveway. Uncle Walter had been something of a hell-raiser in his youth, known for rocketing down the dirt roads at 35 miles an hour. Enthusiastic at barn dances, perhaps he even knocked back a drink or two; certainly he liked the ladies. In fact, their first baby, Wilene—she of the Venetian blinds—weighing 8½ pounds, was born only seven months after Aunt Helen and Uncle Walter were married. Premature, Aunt Helen explained.

Uncle Walter had a pleasant singing voice and at my request would burst into "Sitting in the parlor / In the dimming light" just for me. I can't remember the rest of the words. If he had just come in from the cow barn carrying galvanized pails of fresh milk when we drove in, he'd let me turn the hard-to-turn flywheel on the DeLeval Separator, which, when it got up to humming high speed, spun off thick cream, leaving skimmed milk for the hogs. After that he'd plunk me onto a tall stool for a brisk, no-nonsense haircut. My father was always a bit impatient with Uncle Walter's helter-skelter ways and, I think, judged him an inadequate mate for his favorite sister, also, perhaps, because he'd never managed to own a farm, only sharecrop. Uncle Walter occasionally grumbled that my father was a know-it-all.

Lots of other people dropped into our house in the evenings. Some came to ask my father about wiring buildings or fixing farm machinery; others, such as Henry and Dessie Wachsnicht and their son Howard, came to play cards. But mostly people just came to talk. The men usually sat outside on the wooden porch to exchange stories about farming, or prices, or the weather, or how hard the soil was to plow, or how crops were coming along. In fact, they mostly sat in silence, but then someone would announce: "Why, that field east of the Riek place, it's only makin' about fifteen bushel." Another long silence as we took this in. There was always too much or too little rain, looked like a dry summer, and so on. In the heavy summer air all kinds of insects flocked around the porch light, and further out, hundreds of fireflies filled the night. We kids chased them in the dark, following the tracks of their darting, intermittent flash to take them captive in Mason jars, which, when filled, I imagine must have looked like twinkling lanterns at sea on a dark night.

The women sat inside on rocking chairs, sewing, talking delicately in hushed tones about this or that event or about babies, making clothes, and cooking. I usually started outside on the porch but then came in, perching down on the rug, because the women's conversation was more interesting. All that gossip about people and kids! Besides, the women, particularly Aunt Helen, would lean over the armchair to talk to me while the men never did, except for a bit of kidding. Around ten o'clock, the women produced tea, sandwiches, and cake.

<hr/>

Often, on these summer nights while sitting on the porch, the men stirred, nervous about a sudden calm or the visible churning of dark yellowish purple clouds moving in from the west. Tornadoes were a serious matter even before they were immortalized in the 1939 movie *The Wizard of Oz*. Eight hundred and twenty-nine were recorded in Kansas between the years 1916 and 1954, and the following year, in 1955—I was still away in the air force—one "erased" the south-central town of Udall, killing eighty-two people. Another a few years earlier had wiped out the entire town of Liberal.[2] So we kept a close watch on the sky. When flashes of lightning appeared, the women stayed indoors rocking and sewing while the men and kids went out to the fence west of the house to gauge the possibility of storms or rain. The trick was to get home before the roads got too muddy. After the cars rushed out the driveway, the rumble of deep, rolling thunder and the flash of brilliant sheets of lightning often filled the house. Like everyone else we had a storm cellar but my father absolutely refused to go into it. So we huddled in the southwest corner of the living room, waiting it out, listening to the pelting rain, relieved to hear the thunder move on to the northeast.

The weather in those years before television, like everything else, was completely local. Even though it made no sense in our weather patterns, my mother liked to repeat the maritime refrain:

> "Red sky at night, sailors delight
> Red sky in the morning, sailors take warning."

My father, on the other hand, had two barometers, one of them in the form of a bronze circle embedded together with a thermometer in a varnished wooden plaque that he hung on a nail in the living room wall. Every early evening in the summer we scanned the western horizon for signs. "There's a cloud bank in the west," my father would announce, hopefully if we needed rain or disgustedly if the harvest was under way or if the hay lay in windrows. Of course we had no way of knowing whether this was a narrow band of clouds with miles of clear sky further west or the leading edge of serious weather. We had no ominous warnings on a "weather channel." There were no satellite pictures of whirling clouds over the Philippines or full-figured blondes predicting "shower activity" in the Congo.

The outbreak of war in 1941 diminished the practice of visiting and having company. Gas rationing went into effect, and even though farmers got special allotments for tractors and combines for fuel that could be used in cars, I have the notion that we stayed more at home, had fewer visits. There was, at least in our community, a general sense of austerity, helped no doubt by the lack of things to buy. Factories turned to making tanks and fighter planes, not automobiles; within two months after the Pearl Harbor attack, for example, Ford Motor Company suspended all civilian production. On the other hand, the ever-growing demand for food in war-devastated Europe drove agricultural prices sharply upward. The war years—1941 to 1945—would be golden years for farming in Kansas.

18
War

Just as the drought and the Great Depression were letting up in Kansas, in worlds far distant from ours, two events changed our lives. On September 2, 1939, sister Irene went up to the mailbox at the end of the road to pick up the *Topeka Daily Capitol*. From the kitchen window we saw her running down the driveway, pigtails flying—she was fourteen—crying out, "War, War." The headlines told her that a day earlier the German Army had invaded Poland. A little over two years later on the unseasonably warm afternoon of December 7, 1941, George Riek walked down across the winter-browned alfalfa field from his house to tell us that he'd just heard on the radio about an attack on Pearl Harbor earlier that morning. Our information about those distant places came from the *Daily Capitol*, but by this time we had electricity and a radio, so we could also listen to broadcast news.

Today, when we casually watch an endless succession of global horrors on television, I am struck by my memory of the tremendous impact the news of the distant European and, later, the Pacific war had on all of us. Was it the novelty? In the long, isolated winter nights, did we have no distractions? No kids bounding in from next door to suggest a movie? In the depths of the Kansas countryside, we pored over the *Daily Capitol* and awaited the evening radio news of the European war in high anxiety. We followed over and over the hourly, repetitive broadcasts telling of the Nazi advances through the Low Countries, the collapse of France, and the dramatic evacuation of the British Army at Dunkirk. The same day, Charles Lindbergh, the famed pilot who made the first nonstop Atlantic crossing in *The Spirit of St. Louis* and an enthusiastic admirer of fascism, called for a halt to our "hysterical chatter of calamity of invasion."[1] It all seemed so close. Nowadays, our seemingly endless wars, brought right into the dining room by TV, seem unreal, far away, an abstraction—almost as if they're on the moon.

At age nine, in 1940, I lay awake in my dark upstairs bedroom, having heard downstairs the broadcasts of Edward R. Murrow, worrying myself sick about the threatened invasion of England. I read and memorized parts of Churchill's dramatic speeches to the House of Commons and walked through the barn repeating them out loud in what I must have imagined was a Churchillian voice to an invisible audience. My father, who spoke German until he went to the Schaubel School a half-mile east of the home place, was certainly no Anglophile, but even before the war, he'd acquired a visceral hatred of Adolf Hitler and grimly wagged his head at news of the German advance. At night we listened to broadcasts—and, at my father's insistence, to endless rebroadcasts—of the war news on a much-improved, electric Philco radio. When our protesting clamor reached a high enough pitch, he would relent, and we tuned to *Your Hit Parade*, to comedy shows, to *G-Men*, to Frank Sinatra with Tommy Dorsey and other big bands.

Unlike European and Asian countries that were devastated by invading armies, many of their cities destroyed by the fierce pounding of aerial bombardment, and where millions of soldiers and civilians perished, we experienced the war only indirectly. A Japanese submarine had managed to fire a single harmless shell onto the California shore near an oil refinery, damaging a catwalk; a seaplane dropped a small bomb near the mouth of the Columbia River, destroying a baseball backstop; and toward the end of the war, the Japanese tried to ignite the California and Oregon forests by attaching incendiary devices to balloons that drifted eastward in the prevailing wind, but with no reported effect. On our farm the only case of Japanese aggression we heard about was that of a balloon carrying a small bomb that fell near the end of the war on a farm near Bigelow, a town on the Blue River 20 miles east of our farm. The farmer wanted to keep the balloon to cover his haystack but was persuaded to give it up to the authorities.[2] Apart from a small Japanese force on two tiny islands off the Aleutians, not a single enemy soldier set foot in the United States during World War II. Many Americans, however, including our relatives, died or were wounded fighting abroad. From Clay County alone, 1,416 men and women served in the armed forces in World War II.

Kansas had been an isolationist state after the German invasion of Poland in 1939 and, for that matter, even after England hung by a string during the blitz of 1940. But provoked by the Japanese attack on Pearl Harbor, everyone seems to have sprung into action at once. Within two days after December 7, 1941, 200,000 Kansas men and women—two-fifths of the adult population of the state—signed up for military duty. Kansas was suddenly awash with military contracts for the Wichita companies of Boeing, Beechcraft, and Cessna. Employment at Boeing alone went from 700 workers, many of them women, in 1940 to 29,000 in 1944, and wages were higher than for farmwork: hired hands left farms "in alarming numbers."[3] Overall farm population in Kansas dropped from 607,000 in 1940 to 495,000 by the war's end, driving up farm costs, but prices for what farms produced rose more rapidly. By 1941, wheat brought $1 a bushel and corn 68 cents—the highest prices in a generation. All of us in my family and many of our relatives and neighbors enjoyed more gifts than ever before, including, to my surprise, a new bike (for $24), and the following year, an electric train.

An uncle, several cousins, and many other young men close by enlisted or, more commonly, were drafted into the armed forces of World War II. Parents or wives placed framed stars in their front windows to indicate their men's absence. By the summer of 1942, we began to see ever larger formations of fighter planes flying low over the fields making a terrific racket. Products of the new assembly lines in Wichita, they were heading north, perhaps on training runs, probably destined for the Pacific. These were the first visible, large airplanes to come over our part of Kansas, and whenever the roar began to shake the house, we'd rush outside to gawk aloft. One afternoon, my mother and I, hearing the racket, ran for the door and into the yard to search the sky. Baffled at seeing nothing, we returned to the house and collapsed in laughter. The "engine noises" had come from a war program on the radio.

My cousins and I gathered up and sold the lead panels of discarded storage batteries and scrap iron in Clay Center, not only because everyone seemed to be engaged in the war effort but also because lead and iron brought good money. And about that time, when I was eleven or twelve, my father selected two suckling Hampshire pigs that I might raise as a 4-H project. I devoted special care to them, carrying out pails of skimmed milk, kitchen scraps (pigs will eat anything), and sacks of shelled corn. From sunny spring into the muck of winter the nameless piglets grew into large, friendly creatures, half farm animal and half pet. In mid-December we trucked them off to a local market. They sold for about $40 apiece. What was I to do with the unheard-of proceeds of this tender, loving care? A Christmas present, perhaps, for myself? It may sound smug, but actually, I bought each of my parents a war bond that would mature in ten years at $50.

⇒◆⇐

The war years in general, however devastating to uncounted countries and millions of soldiers and civilians across the planet, were benign and ultimately profitable for those of us able to stay at home; at least that was the case for our and our neighbors' farms in eastern Kansas. The rains returned, the dust settled; with little to buy we were forced to save and by mid-1941, prices for the things we produced rose steadily even after the bonanza of 1941, and by the end of the war they had nearly doubled for most farm products while our costs rose slowly.

It was also true that because industry turned to the manufacture of tanks, planes, and ships, new farm machinery—particularly tractors, combined harvesters, corn pickers, and trucks—was scarce. And so were farmworkers. First of all, nearly 16 million men and women served in the army, navy, and marine corps during the war, and millions more were employed in war-related jobs. Women were recruited for farm labor, and several thousand workers from Mexico came to work in Kansas fields. This scarcity of field hands may explain why I underwent forced recruitment to full-time worker in the fields at age eleven or twelve, and why my sisters, both in high school, spent their girlish summers tending cattle and shocking wheat.

In August 1945, after the deaths of more than 60 million people, the war ended. A month later, my father drove me off from the farm one September morning to engage the daunting mysteries of the 300-strong student body of Clay County Community High School, two events, it must have felt to me, of nearly equal magnitude.

19
Town and Country

The reader of these stories about the countryside and farms might get the impression that towns and cities were of little importance to our lives; but in fact, there was a real city, Kansas City, Missouri, 175 miles east, at the confluence of the Kansas and Missouri rivers. Kansas City was famous in the nineteenth century as a stepping-off place for the western movement of pioneers, trappers, and Indian fighters; later, its vast stockyards were rivaled only by those in Chicago; and for a time, in the 1930s, the city was made notorious by gangsters pursued by J. Edgar Hoover's G-men, and by a corrupt and highly successful city boss, Tom Pendergast. In my youthful imagination there were Very Tall Buildings in Kansas City, unimagined crowds of people, big stores, and a famed hotel, the Muehlebach, that of course we never entered and that the men only mentioned in hushed, admiring tones at home.

In my early teens, I was permitted to accompany our neighbor Harold Riek, the driver of a truckload of our fattened steers, to Kansas City. We stayed in the stockyards district, only two or three streets from the blocks and blocks—it seemed like miles and miles— of wooden pens teeming with jostling and bellowing cattle. We found a hotel, the Missouri Hotel, a place I then thought overwhelmingly grand but was surprised to find several years later was a two-floor walk-up with tattered carpets and peeling wallpaper. That evening in the nearby diner I overheard two men in the adjoining booth engaged in what I took to be hushed, conspiratorial, gangster talk about Pretty Boy Floyd and the "Kansas City Massacre." It was probably only ordinary discussion about a newspaper story. Listening too much to the dramatic, sirens-wailing radio program *G-Men* inflamed one's youthful imagination.

My parents occasionally—perhaps once or twice a year—drove our Oldsmobile the four or five hours to Kansas City, accompanying truckloads of cattle or hogs to the stockyards. Usually the Hofmanns or Aunt Helen and Uncle Walter went along with them. This was not an occasion, as one might imagine today, for shopping, sightseeing, a movie, a play or "dining out," but merely "for the drive." But my sisters and I did learn, through overheard conversation, that on one occasion, at least, our parents had taken in a vaudeville show. When pressed for details, my mother, who had worn her best dress to the show, described the experience rather gingerly, with a shy edge of embarrassment. Another time, in the middle of the war, when blackouts were imposed on such unlikely targets for Nazi bombers as Kansas City, another neighbor, Henry Wachsnicht, returned from a cattle-shipping trip. I asked him whether "the curfew was on" when he was there. "My goodness," he said, "I never got a chance to go to that."

These rather oblique and vicarious accounts of The City, as Kansas City, Missouri, was known, left us with an incomplete, tantalizing, and somewhat apprehensive picture of the distant metropolis.

<hr/>

"Town" for us meant Clay Center, the seat of Clay County, founded in 1862 by brothers Alonzo and John Dexter, who were originally from Maine. Striking it rich during the gold rush years, they brought $25,000 in gold from California to get things going, laid out the town plat, named streets (a central one for themselves), and opened the first modest stores. Even so, ten years later in 1873, this was still a frontier town. An account that year noticed "an absence of class feeling"; all the town people "were poor, struggling to exist, and willing to share with each other the pleasures and privations of pioneer life."[1]

But that quickly changed. The arrival of intercontinental railroads brought eastern markets within reach and pumped money into Kansas' agricultural economy. In the early 1880s, Kansans harvested an annual wheat crop of 25 million bushels.[2]

The people of Clay County, of course, participated in the good times, but the new prosperity was felt unevenly across the town and countryside. In the course of a single decade, Clay Center was rapidly modernized. By 1886, water-powered dynamos generated power for its first electric lights while farms had to wait more than a half-century for the REA. Even smaller towns, like Green and Morganville, did not have electricity until the World War I era. The same year that electric lights arrived in Clay Center, four new streetcars ran on steel tracks through the streets. A bit later, sewers were opened (employing a large number of migrant "tramps" as workers), and most houses acquired indoor plumbing.[3] Telephones came in 1897, and "wires filled the air, reaching houses everywhere, even strung from tree to tree and between houses."[4] In 1901, builders brought the excellent building material "Manhattan stone" from quarries 40 miles away and laid the cornerstone for one of the most impressive small-town courthouses in the state that still stands.

Some farmers acquired better reapers and threshers, others improved their barns and houses; but for most, their daily life was only slightly changed. No electricity on the farm meant no refrigeration, running water, or indoor toilets, and the use of dim kerosene lamps to light house and barns continued. In Clay County the 160-acre homestead worked by family labor and horsepower still prevailed; roads remained rustic in good weather and impassable in bad.

———✦———

Here then, in the last two decades of the nineteenth century, is when a wide breach opened between town and country, a split that could still be seen—and felt—well into the 1940s and early 1950s.

Clay Center, by this time, was a place of some 8,000 people with handsome, flourishing, commercial streets around the Courthouse Square. A large, square post office and a solid Carnegie Library, both made of tan bricks, occupied the streets opposite the square. Three banks stood at the corner of the main intersection; one of them had what appeared to be bullet scars on the marble name plaque, the result, according to local lore—probably not true—of a foiled attempt at robbery in the Depression years. There were two movie houses, the Star and the Rex; two pool halls, one called the Idle Hour; three or four gasoline filling stations out on Highways 24 and 15; several clothing and farm supply stores; a large grain elevator; two hardware stores;

three or four simple diners (where we might be treated, "once in a blue moon," to chicken-fried steak, roast beef in gravy, and mashed potatoes); two drugstores with soda fountains; and Carlies Ice Cream.

There were a number of doctors and dentists, including Dr. Johnson, who pulled or drilled your teeth (without anesthetic). In contrast—on the farm—if the pain of a rotten tooth became unbearable, a neighbor might be persuaded to bring out his pliers to solve the problem. Clay Center had a large, two-story community hospital and three rather grand primary schools. Finally, the largest edifice in town, attended by some 300 students, was the handsome three-story Clay County Community High School, complete with gymnasium, basketball court, football practice field, and even paved courts for tennis, a game utterly unknown in the countryside. The municipal swimming pool represented another rural-urban gap. We swam in the muddy streams of Fancy and Carter creeks; town kids leapt with glee into a state-of-the-art, 230,000-gallon municipal swimming pool that had been opened in 1934.

During the years we're talking about—the 1940s and 50s—both the Rock Island railroad and the main line of the transcontinental Kansas Pacific passed through Clay Center on their way to Kansas City and beyond. Sometimes, rarely, we were in town as the train came through. That was a big event. You could hear in the distance the rumble of the long procession of boxcars pulled by huge black steam locomotives, listen intently as the train grew closer, and then stand rapt at the crossing as it thundered through town.

On one occasion, my father dropped me off from the car at the Nelson brothers fur traders to haggle over the price of my year's catch of muskrat pelts. The fur trader had his store, a large, heavy-timbered open room with a sliding door, on a platform that faced, and was almost within reach of, the tracks. The place stunk of dried animal skins and grease. In the midst of our discussions—it's surprising to me now that my father wasn't present—a huge freight train that seemed, and most likely was, a mile long roared by, shaking the platform so that I braced myself against the wall, more than a little anxious.

From first settlement down to World War I, many individual farm families traveled to Clay Center and back in horse-drawn wagons or buggies. This meant that you had to leave early in the day to be home by nightfall, and consequently, trips were very rare. The further out the farm, the fewer the trips to town. By the 1920s, most farm families had simple cars, and a bit later headlights, barely adequate, were common. The counties bought graders to smooth the rutted, often uneven dirt roads. The north-south State Highway 15 was graded and the east-west U.S. Highway 24 paved. Nevertheless, we rarely went into Clay Center. But by the later 1940s if there were no pressing tasks at home, or if rain kept us out of the fields, or if the harvest or plowing were finished, on Saturday nights my family would "go to town." I tagged along as my mother and sisters in their plain dresses and shoes strolled down the principal streets, browsed in the Five and Ten, and looked in at Duckwall's General Merchandise and the hardware store to buy a tin cupcake form or set of iced tea glasses. It seemed to me that they were forever running into other people or families from neighboring farms to gossip and exchange information on gardens and canning, on babies and illness. I imagine I tugged impatiently on Mother's long arms, but I also remember when very young an anxious fear of separation and getting lost in the teeming multitudes in the streets. Farther down Court Street, my father leaned longingly on the new harvesters in the W. W. Smith & Sons farm machinery store and talked solemnly with other farmers about the weather and soils.

—————

The reason we rarely went to town was that there were only a few things we could buy or, for that matter, needed to buy; farms and towns constituted quite different universes. That's because farms were pretty much self-sufficient, and the wheat and cattle that we sold directly from the farm were usually trucked to local grain elevators or to the stockyards in Kansas City. We sold grain, mostly wheat, oats and corn, and cattle and pigs on the hoof. Mother sold eggs gathered and stacked in molded paper flats, two dozen to the flat, twelve flats deep, in large, reusable wooden boxes and poured thick cream in 5-gallon heavy metal cans. Trucks from a company called The Linn Creamery picked up both. The income from this was hers, used for cash purchases of cloth, clothes, shoes, and the odd household item. Before my father began to wire houses and do custom hay baling, these "exports" were the main source of our household income.

Compared with all the things we buy today, our purchases then, either from mail-order catalogues, such as Montgomery Ward or Sears & Roebuck, or from Clay Center, were scant. The farm supplied nearly all our food. My father kept a close accounting of income and expenses in a formal ledger during these years, which I came across only after he died. It shows that the only things we regularly bought in town were coffee, sugar, shoes, and overalls. The ledger also shows the different kinds of cloth out of which mother made shirts and dresses on the treadle-driven Singer sewing machine.

All adult men had a proper suit with dress shirt, tie, and a felt hat for weddings and funerals, usually kept for years; a "good" pair of shoes; and heavy wool coats against the cold. Both men and women bought their own and their children's dress and work shoes and work clothes. My mother made my shirts and ordinary dresses and pajamas for my sisters, but, like the men, she bought factory-made underwear. I imagine the largest expenses went for farm supplies: hoes, scythes, pitchforks, saws, axes, knives of various kinds, all kinds of wrenches and other tools for machinery, oil and gas, nails and bolts. But most such items lasted a long time and required yearly, not weekly or even monthly, trips to Clay Center.

By the end of World War II the Depression and drought had also passed. Too young for the First World War and too old for the Second, my father, with the voluntary labor of a single son, became a bit better off. In 1945 he acquired a new Case hay baler, one of the first to be had after the country turned from tanks and planes to cars and farm machinery, together with a small used tractor, and we began to go around the country doing "custom" hay baling. My father sat on one side feeding the baling wires through metal channels between the bales. I sat opposite, tying the wires. The tractor pulled us along in clouds of dust, while the baler's spiked pickup machinery often stirred up nests of furious bumblebees. This work, along with all the usual work of plowing, planting, and harvest, occupied our summers from early morning to nightfall, except for the rare rainy day. On a good day we might put out 1,000 bales of alfalfa or prairie hay, which meant $100 gross income for the family, which, along with the sale of grain and livestock, although still modest, made up a veritable fortune. My father charged 10 cents a bale; the tractor driver got 1 cent, the son nothing. A well-known economist, Alexander Chayanov, a student of serfdom, believed that in prerevolutionary Russia, fathers exploited their own children more effectively than did the masters their serfs.

When the autumn hay season ended, my father had all sorts of houses and outbuildings lined up for wiring. In 1946, he bought a new four-door Ford and soon after, a new Ford pickup truck (and then, an electric sewing machine for mother).

Around this time, my family went more frequently to Clay Center. Bogart's, the first large "supermarket"—actually a one-room, curved-roof shed—offered loaves of sliced, soft, tasteless bread, which we loved; slightly tired vegetables and fruit appeared even during the winter. As we drove down the residential streets in the summertime, we'd notice the town people themselves often sitting in swings on their porches watching as we passed by gawking at their substantial houses and lawn sprinklers. In the downtown streets there was an array of new stores and shiny new goods. Sometimes we'd be treated to nickel hamburgers in a little corner diner next to the filling station, a welcome change from fresh fried chicken and tender ears of corn that were the standard fare at home. I wouldn't go near a Big Mac today, but the smell of grease frying on the flat tin grill, the oil-paper burger wrappers, and the feel of the torn plastic covers on the counter stools still call out to me to this day.

The more powerful cars with good headlights and more miles of graded, graveled, and even paved roads encouraged farm families to go more frequently to Clay Center. Higher farm prices put more money in their pockets and there were more things to buy. Saturday night shopping or just mingling in the crowded streets became a near-universal ritual. From the 1950s onward the inexorable decline of farms and the smaller number of rural people, together with the coming of that marvelous and irresistible device, television, began to change all this. The fluorescence of Clay Center and the Saturday night community came to an end. The town people left their porch swings and went inside, the farm people stayed home. By the late 1950s you could have rolled a bowling ball down the main street on Saturday night without scattering a single soul: they were all indoors, at home, glued to the flickering TV, watching Lawrence Welk or Liberace or the news, and certainly the weather.

———

The years between the end of one war (1945) and the beginning of another (in Korea, 1950) were also my high school years. It will be hard for readers of this book, and it's even hard for me, to remember how different towns were from the farms. In my memories of the 1930s and 40s, Clay Center was a distant and strange place populated by people who talked, dressed, and even looked quite different. The gulf that separated farmers from town people was especially noticeable between farm and town *kids*, even, as in this case, when the town was hardly a sophisticated metropolis but rather a small county seat of 8,000 souls. For one thing, the 15 miles over indifferent roads between our farm and town meant that we lived lives quite isolated from town. My father may have gone to Clay Center for repairs or electrical supplies every three or four weeks but I, either in school or occupied with chores, rarely went along. Besides, we were basically self-sufficient in food, bought few clothes, and were certainly not accustomed to going to movies; so in the 1930s and early 40s we had only a glimpse of Clay Center on Saturday night, if at all.

The big challenge for me came with high school. Town kids were no longer the ones we eyed suspiciously through the car window but were now sitting side by side with us in classrooms and obviously knew a lot more about how the world worked than we did. They also knew each other, having attended the three large primary schools in town, and went around in familiar groups. I only knew Donnie Hofmann and two or three cousins from other school districts. The town kids wore what seemed to me very fancy clothes, most store-bought, of course. They talked differently from us, used slang words I'd never heard and can't remember now, and they had not only seen, but had actually played, football and basketball games in primary school.

My father drove me to Clay Center that first day at Clay County Community High School (CCCHS) and thereafter I would either ride into Clay Center and home again after school with Donnie Hofmann in his Model A Ford or, in case of bad weather, stay with Grandma Bauer, who had moved to town a few years after Grandfather William died. The high school had three entrances. The main one, where most students entered, was crowded with town kids greeting each other the first day of class after the long summer with yelps of recognition, laughing and joking, examining each other's clothes. They stood in circles, occasionally looking back over their shoulders at the rustic fauna just then being dropped off by their farm parents, pointing and giggling . . . at least that's how I remember it now.

There were also two longer diagonal solitary paths leading through the cover of shrubs to the side entrances. I nervously asked my father to drop me at one of these paths rather than plunge into the intimidating crowd further down.

"Why not down there?" He gave me a stern sideways look. Had he sensed my embarrassment at our mud-spattered car and my own clothes and work shoes? Crossing my arms over the plain brown shirt with the large collar and huge white buttons that my mother had made for the occasion, I made my way down the diagonal path, past the bewildering halls of CCCHS, and then into the intimidating melee of classrooms and unfamiliar young people. At the end of that first day, by the time I'd attended the afternoon classes, I still walked with my arms crossed in front of my chest to hide the embarrassment of the brown shirt.

Was that true? Was it really like that? Do the few surviving town kids today remember it like that? Hard to know. But I don't think that the self-segregation of town and farm kids was entirely my imagination. All of my high school friends during the first two years were farm kids. I tried to befriend Dwight Adams, a lawyer's son, I believe, who always sat in the seat just ahead of me (we were seated alphabetically in classrooms), but while polite, he went his own way after class, moving in other circles.

Sports, a potential site for interaction and making friends, presented another rural-urban barrier. I was told in the first few days of orientation that tennis courts were available (!) and that we could "go out" for the football or basketball teams, but since I had never seen one of those games, I had little chance to make either team. Town kids had played together in their primary schools and I later learned that their parents had even taken them to see college games at Kansas State College. The only team sports that country kids played were baseball and softball, but the high school offered no program in those games.

I don't remember choosing classes that first fall, but I imagine advisors guided us through the various options during the following two years. I do remember a discouraging C in Mrs. Reynolds's history class, writing adequate essays in English, and the complete horror of having to stand before thirty other students in Mrs. Perkins's speech class (required) and tell a story. I chose to tell of my parents missing a county road sign and running into a ditch. This, one might say, fell flat and provoked more giggles. Even with the daily distraction of Dixie Chapman's smooth bare shoulders in the seat just ahead (the alphabetical order must have been relaxed), I did OK in Mr. McClenahan's geometry class. The school offered Latin, and Mr. Snodgrass, the music teacher, formed a school orchestra. No one I knew took those courses. My favorite class was shop, where I was able to make concrete hog troughs and case-hardened steel chisels, and a woodworking class where I made an impressive bed with lathe-turned legs and quite beautiful head- and footboards from the cedar and walnut trees sawed by my father in the mill he'd made to survive the Depression.

Then there was the business of girls, especially town girls, and one's disquieting libido. There were girls, too, of course, out on the farms, but strangely enough, despite the fact that farms and families were pretty thick on the ground at that time, there were few occasions to get together with them. There were few girls my age and only four or five in Fairfield School District #24. I can't remember any neighborhood or birthday parties or church social events, or even imagine dances. Except for the Parent/Teacher night when I "picked up Joan Dankenbring," there were few other opportunities to experience or enjoy close company with another girl. The most confusing and innocent erotic feelings broke out in all sorts of places. *Life* magazine's cover picture of Judy Garland left my mouth hanging open; Lana Turner in a provocative pose with John Garfield, worse yet.

So, in the postwar fall of 1945, I found myself in the social whirl of Clay Center with little preparation for socializing with the other sex, let alone knowing anything about the rituals of dating, and less about combat in the erogenous zone. Here, town kids went out on dates, went to dances, some sponsored by various churches; they talked excitedly about the latest movies at the Rex and Star theatres downtown, hung out at the soda fountain, and found the distance from the front porch to the backseat only a short leap.[5] I can't remember a single date in the first two, maybe three years at CCCHS. That seems to me now quite pathological but I believe it wasn't uncommon and was explained in part, at least, by the rural-urban cultural divide. Dance? I'd never danced. Here, everyone was doing the jitterbug. Go out on "dates"? Not much practice for that on the farm. Where would we have gone on a date, to a hayloft? Donnie Hofmann was the only kid who had his own car, and he wouldn't have let anyone else behind the wheel.

Then, too, some town girls seemed to fall quickly into the new category of "teenager," a term invented, presumably, by the big-city advertising and marketing agencies (in the 1940s?) to create a new consumer category. The more advanced town girls read *Seventeen*, first published in 1944, went around together dressed in clothes appropriate to "teenagers," and got on the Honor Roll for high grades. All very intimidating. There were no "teenagers" on the farm. From seven to eighteen we—boys and girls alike—worked along a continuum from simple to more useful worker. Nor was there a break in style or kind of clothing. I notice in photographs that I wore the same blue-and-white-striped overalls for my first birthday picture as I did for the sixteenth.

By the third year in high school the differences between the town and farm kids began to blur. I'd managed to become a third-string substitute on the CCCHS Tigers football team; I think my grades picked up a bit. And during the fourth year, I even went out on dates with the incredibly beautiful and sophisticated Joyce Jevons, a daughter of the manager of the Jevons Appliance Store, described in the 1949 yearbook as "a happy girl with golden hair, brown eyes, a good student and thoughtful of others." Joyce sold tickets sitting in the kiosk out front of the Rex movie house, and sometimes, when I had my parents' car, I'd drive by just to get a look at her. She was unaware of my lonely passion, but now and then permitted me to pick her up after the show, at ten o'clock or so, for an ice cream at Carlies and then to drive her home. I actually considered inviting her out to the farm to meet my parents, but the thought of that girl making her way over the uneven path to the outhouse, and the splintery wooden seat, erased that notion.

Cut from the football team in my senior year, I was freed to travel to out-of-town games in Abilene, Concordia, and Salina with Joyce and other couples. Several town kids had cars, so we'd pile in—driver and date up front, four in the back—the intoxicating and very sophisticated scent of Evening in Paris, Joyce's favorite perfume, wafting up among us. Toward the end of our senior year, she and I were together in a school play and also members of the high school's "Model United Nations" program. Some malevolent gossips called Joyce "the fastest girl in town." She wasn't "fast," alas, with me. I can't imagine why she asked me, a klutzy nondancer, to the Senior Prom, but she did.

I've often wondered if she ever thought of me, of that soft summer night when I drove her home after the prom. There was a tender kiss in the car. She stepped out, removed her high-heeled shoes with one hand, gathered the orchid corsage—*de rigueur* for the prom—with the other, and carefully picked her way barefoot across the garden to her parents' house where the porch light had been left on. At the door she turned, held up the two shoes in a playful farewell gesture, gave me a sweet smile, and disappeared inside. I drove off in my parents' 1949 Ford. My high school days were over.

Only a few months ago, at a high school reunion, I heard that Joyce had died several years ago in California. Cancer. She's dead, that Golden Girl is dead. And so is our youth and those soft nights, when, as someone said, many things were so new that they still lacked names.

20
Leaving Home

The summer after graduating from high school in June 1949, I stayed on the farm. My father had acquired another 160 acres, a new tractor, and a better hay baler for custom work on other farms, so with the daily chores, ordinary care of machinery and animals, there were plenty of things to do. When we were not in the fields, or after work in the evenings or occasionally on Sundays, I'd drive our new '49 Ford into Clay Center to meet up with the friends I'd made in school. We'd play snooker at the Idle Hour pool hall, have a glass or two of tap beer, drive slowly and aimlessly around the town, have an ice cream at Carlies, and be home by 10 p.m.

If rain dampened the windrows of alfalfa or made the fields muddy, my young friends or cousins and I might fish for catfish in Fancy Creek or even sally forth for picnics along the rivers of neighboring towns. On one occasion, cruising in Clay Center, we'd come across three girls from Concordia, a few miles to the northwest, who invited us to join them camping out on a low sandy island in the middle of the Republican River. All three girls smoked and seemed remarkably sophisticated, a bit intimidating. To get up to speed, I bought my first pack of Camels, practiced lighting up in the rearview mirror of the Ford in preparation for the encounter, and that Saturday the six of us lay all the warm night on blankets on the island, I enjoying the incredibly soft kisses of the friendliest of the three sophisticates. Driving back, we listened to Nat King Cole singing "Mona Lisa." Eighteen years old. The war in the past, a new car to drive, feeling my oats.

Once a week I played first base on the blue-uniformed "Dynamos" softball team under the lights at Huntress Park in Clay Center. My single athletic triumph was the boyhood American dream. Two on, one out, my team trailing 3 to 5, the last half of the final inning against a superior visiting team. I came to bat. The first two high-rising fastball pitches were wide—I can still see them; the third I hit into the trees beyond left field, my only home run of the season. Afterward, several of us, still in uniform, drove to Green where the annual carnival and community picnic was in full swing. I strode though the crowd of friends and relatives feeling—or as close as I've ever come to feeling—as I imagined Stan the Man might feel after hitting one out of old Sportsman's Park.

<hr/>

But what now? Continue to work with my father on the farm? Go to college? No one in my extended family had ever gone to college or knew what went on in such a place. My parents had not gone beyond the eighth grade; it was a universe unknown to them. The father of Raymond Vadnais, however, one of my high school friends, was a farm machinery salesman who had attended Kansas State College. Ray occasionally invited me to his house in Clay Center. His mother became fond of me, and since Ray intended to follow in his father's footsteps to Kansas State, Mr. Vadnais and his wife encouraged me to apply as well. Somehow, despite my mediocre high school performance, I was accepted and that autumn enrolled in Kansas State to study agricultural engineering, something that sounded appropriate, maybe useful. My parents did not object to this turn of events, although my father might reasonably have had mixed feelings at the prospect of losing an able-bodied worker.

Raymond, the only person I knew in Manhattan, was lined up to live in his father's fraternity. I found a bed in the third-floor attic of a large house several blocks from campus that I came to share with three other students for $25 a month; the accommodations included a refrigerator, a two-burner hot plate, and simple plates, knives, and forks. I struggled mightily and often despairingly with beginning courses in algebra, chemistry, and English. In a shop course, I learned to cast molten aluminum into a form, making an ashtray with a raised letter B in the base. I still have the ashtray.

On most weekends in the fall and following spring, I found a ride, or hitchhiked up Highway 24 to Clay Center, and then found my way out to the farm for a weekend of work. My feet may have been in Manhattan but my head was still on the farm. I can't remember any friends from that first college year, beyond the three attic mates, and the occasional chat on campus with Raymond. I hadn't bowled over my teachers at K-State, finishing the school year with barely a C average and a warning letter from the dean addressed—to my enormous embarrassment—to my parents, pointing out the depressing record and warning of expulsion if I didn't shape up. Curiously, my mother was disturbed; my father said not a word. At the end of the school term, in May 1950, I moved out of the attic bed, gathered my books and clothes in a suitcase, and returned home. Raymond said, rather encouragingly, that if I returned in the fall, he might be able to persuade his fraternity to accept me.

⎯⎯•⎯⎯

Back on the farm, I got in the swing of farmwork, ventured into Clay Center for pool and beer. During the first few weeks of the softball season, my team, the Dynamos, had qualified for a regional tournament in Great Bend, a town some three hours by car to the southwest of Clay Center. To my surprise, my father indicated his interest in driving the new Ford out there to watch the game, and so, on June 25, 1950, my mother and father, along with Aunt Helen and Uncle Walter and I, made our way out Highway 156 to Great Bend. Alas, the Dynamos were eliminated in the first round by a fireballing black pitcher whose deliveries seemed to rise from his shoe tops to the plate at hurricane speed. Why do I remember this game? Because I got one of our two hits, a bloop single to right. Had I been aware of metaphor, that feeble triumph might have served to describe my year at Kansas State. That evening, driving home from Great Bend, we heard on the car radio that North Korean troops had invaded South Korea. I couldn't know it then, but the invasion and the subsequent war would change everything.

I decided not to return to Kansas State for the fall term and for the rest of the summer and early fall I lived on the farm, falling back into the familiar routine. I helped harvest the wheat, plowed and disked the stubble, baled hay, fed the cattle, and listened—no TV yet—to the weather and ten o'clock news every night. I discussed casually with my father the possibility of going back down to Kansas State next year and maybe becoming a farm agent. He asked how long such a course of study would take and where I'd most likely settle in Kansas afterward, and if such a job paid "good money." I remember feeling that on the whole he was skeptical of such a plan, and when I asked what he thought I might do, he replied, "Why, I don't know, that's up to you," and then to my surprise, he added, "I never thought you'd stay home." What did he imagine? How would I make a living? Stay on the farm? My sisters were definitely, scornfully, opposed to that.

What *should* I do? I wasn't keen to go back down to Kansas State; it had not exactly been a rewarding experience. My former high school classmates were scattering out. Quite a few got jobs in Clay Center, one in a furniture store, another working out on Highway 15 at the gas station. A doctor's son, a kid in my class, was entering KU. Jim Grogan, the high school quarterback, got a fellowship from some small college back east. Would the new war affect my life? Two cousins had already been drafted. The news seemed more ominous every night, and even though I shared everyone's opinion that the Communists had to be stopped, I wasn't ready to rush out to enlist. Besides, I liked the hot summer nights watching the lightning bugs flicker along as I sat on the east porch, liked playing softball with the former high school buddies who were still around, having a beer or two at the Idle Hour afterward. Now and then I even went out with a girlfriend of sorts, in the form of Emma, an "older woman" of some twenty-three years who taught school in Green.

What should I do? What *could* I do? I didn't know how to think about that question. What did other young people *do*, anyway? What alternatives were there? I could, of course, stay on the farm—at least temporarily—I thought. Even my precocious sister Irene had the same problem: what do all those people out there do? She must not have known either, since the first year out of high school, in 1942, she took a job in a rural school just a few miles from our farm at $65 a month. It was the most inappropriate thing imaginable for my high-spirited sister with an eye on a more distant horizon, and after one year, she was up and away.

In October, the war news became much worse. Chinese soldiers crossed the Yalu River into North Korea. We all knew that the Communists—Chinese, Russians, whatever—were bent on world conquest and that things were really heating up. I drove into Clay Center and climbed the stairs to a small office to see the man who worked at the Draft Board.

"Where am I on the list?" I asked.

"Let's see," he said, running his finger down a list of names in the ledger. "Why, you're number two, just after your cousin here."

I drove home, informed my parents that I was going to enlist in the air force. My father exhibited mixed emotions—pride and sudden worry about who would help with the corn picking. My mother was devastated. I felt relieved; my immediate future, at least, was suddenly resolved.

The air force "processed" me through Kansas City; there was an overnight train journey to Lackland AFB in Texas, where I underwent basic training; then to Keesler AFB in Biloxi, Mississippi, for nearly a year of electronic training and security checks; then to Sandia Base near Albuquerque, New Mexico. In November 1952, my specialized and top-secret unit of the Armed Forces Special Weapons Command crossed the country to New York City where I boarded the USS *General Hodges* for Casablanca, then still-*French* Morocco.

My group, made up of a dozen enlisted men, six officers, and a large number of well-armed security people, was assigned the responsibility of maintaining and setting the radar fusing devices of what we now know as "Weapons of Mass Destruction," in our case in the form of Mark VI atomic bombs kept in deep underground concrete bunkers near an American air base some 20 miles outside of Casablanca. In our normal routine, Boeing B-47 Stratojet bombers touched down unannounced onto the runways at any time of day or night. Our unit's task was to leap from our cots, hit the ground running, and load the preprogrammed bombs into the planes that, with engines screaming, pressed against the wheel blocks before roaring off, thereby keeping aloft at all times the threat of a nuclear strike on our godless Cold War enemy.

The two years in Morocco, including travel in postwar Europe, exposure to an exotic culture in the throes of an anticolonial struggle, and the chance to spend time in a different language with people very different from me, led me to discover a person I didn't know existed. I entered those two years as a naive, uneducated Kansas farm kid and emerged as a still-uneducated farm kid with a different set of naiveties, but also as a young person open to the horizons of a wider world that—for better or for worse—led me to leave the farm.

Casablanca was my "bend in the river." On December 13, the USS *General Hodges* docked in the harbor of what was then Africa's third largest city, and a week later I took the air force shuttle bus into the city to find a table lamp. It was my first close-up of a foreign city, and I quickly discovered the meaning of a "language barrier." *No one* spoke English; it took all afternoon to buy a table lamp; moreover, the city was full of beggars and thieves and swarms of Arab youths who practically tore me limb from limb at the bus station. I am surprised now to read in the diary I kept during those years that a week after the table lamp adventure, I—who had never spoken or read a word in a foreign language—enrolled in a conversational French course on the air base and a couple of months later managed to find the widow of a French officer, one Mme. Belouet, who gave tutorials in her apartment, "trente-trois, rue de la Salle, Casablanca," as I wrote in my diary, April 12, 1952.

In the course of the following two years, even with imperfect French, I found that I could move with growing ease into that exotic city. I struck up a friendship with a French soldier, whose battalion would be devastated at Dien Bien Phu in Vietnam; sought out friendly barmaids to practice the language; pursued another friendly young Frenchman I'd met in a sidewalk café to talk on three or four occasions about "Franco-American relations." I shudder to think now of the jejune content of those meetings, but still I wrote in my diary, "There is so much to be gained by living and knowing another culture for a time. I so enjoy talking to the French, getting their ideas, etc." With one or two fellow airmen I traveled to the ancient cities of Fez and Marrakesh and spent as much time as I could in Casablanca. As we went along I even became the more or less official, if imperfect, translator of the odd love letter written by local girls to my barrack mates, widening my vocabulary into more intimate realms.

In May 1953, Malcolm, my best friend in our unit, a talented young man who had studied geology at Stanford, met, courted, and married a young Spanish girl, the daughter of Spanish Republican exiles, whose father had been murdered by the Fascists in Seville in 1936. The social events surrounding the courtship and the wedding party itself gave me the entry to family life, the possibility of learning something about Spain and of meeting young women: date, eat, drink, even dance.

Here's my diary entry for December 2, 1953: "Had one of the most enjoyable evenings of my young life last night. Birthday party for Teresa at the Café Sevilla. They rolled out the carpet for us, people danced on tabletops, etc., there was a very pretty Spanish girl there called Angélica, 'qui a les plus jolies jambes de l'Afrique du Nord.'"

About this time, if my social life flourished, my conventional—if unexamined—patriotism received a body blow. Brought up in a time and place of staunch conservative values, I had entered the air force as a convinced cold warrior. I was pleased that General Eisenhower had become president; I knew little of Senator McCarthy's work on rooting out Communists from our government, but had I known, I doubt I'd have disapproved. My diary records pride in our Special Weapons unit as a main defense against the "Kremlin hordes." Then, one afternoon, deep in one of the underground bunkers, lying on the broad back of a Mark VI atomic bomb, my feet braced up on the tail fins, I came across an interview with our secretary of state in the Defense Department's newspaper, *Stars and Stripes*. Mr. Dulles was quoted as saying that "the United States has not now, and has no intention, of placing nuclear weapons in North Africa." I was astonished. Deeply offended. "How could my government lie to me!"

All of this—the partial, at least, immersion in the exotic life of Casablanca, a beginning knowledge of another language, the growing anticolonial revolution that one saw from the taxi or bus windows, and not least, the unexpected and generous charms of Angélica— inevitably changed the way I thought about things. I recorded a hint of my ingenuous sophistication in the diary entry of January 24, 1953: "Lt. Price when talking about Europe remarked that the French seemed lazy. It is disturbing how few Americans try to understand the Europeans' way of thinking. We cannot fathom how much suffering and disappointment they have gone through in the past fifty years, having wars destroy their countries. They do not want sympathy from us nor do they want to live as we do."

Another six months and we were back on the USS *General Hodges* for our return to New Jersey and discharge from the air force. Diary entry, July 8, 1954: "Will now pack this Diary in preparation for the sea passage. We leave this Sunday ending 27 months tour." And then, August 17, 1954: "Have spent the last three weeks at home. Bought a 1950 Ford with money saved in Air Force, worked with Dad on the farm, lots of baling hay and plowing, visited friends and relatives. Applied for my GI Bill benefit and passport. I am going to Mexico City College. I've been accepted."

⇒•⇐

My mother was uncomprehending but unopposed to my plan for Mexico City. She couldn't have known much, and may never have heard of that country. She must have thought that, even if I didn't stay on the farm, I wouldn't be far away; perhaps I'd go back down to Kansas State or find a job with Boeing Airplane Company in Wichita, something I'd casually mentioned. I didn't want to imagine her distraught nights: did she lie tearfully alongside my sleeping father, or even harder to imagine, did they both quietly wonder about my plans, about what it would all mean?

My father must have expected me to stay for a time on the farm— at least until I had figured out what I was going to do with my life. I'm sure he thought I'd stay in Kansas, and most certainly in the country. After all, I was the only son and the last of his family at home. It's not that we discussed my leaving; my father was not a man to put his arm on your shoulder for a cozy talk. It's also true that after returning from the air force and Morocco, we had our "issues"— political and personal storms that blew up with disproportionate fury over the breakfast table or after listening to the evening news. When I first screwed up my courage to declare that I was going to Mexico City, he asked, "So what's the matter, don't they have schools good enough for you in this country?"

Even given our differences, that was a harsh remark. Was it just disappointment? Could he have felt envy? Did he sense then the paradox that's only now apparent to me: that his own broad interests, unusual for that time and place, eventually spurred me to leave for a foreign land? My father was only able to attend the eight grades of the local school, but during my and my sisters' early years on the farm, he subscribed—in what must have been an extravagant luxury—to *Look, Life, National Geographic, The Saturday Evening Post,* and other magazines that piled up in a rack next to the radio. From these and from the world news, some of the awareness of the wider world and a desire to experience it must have seeped into my subconscious. My sister Irene was a more conscious model. Four years out of high school, she found her way into a secretarial job with General McArthur's staff in Tokyo and then enjoyed a long career in the American Foreign Service, ending up as personnel officer in the Athens Embassy.

I stayed for six more weeks on the farm, plowing, baling alfalfa and prairie grass, and helping with the chores. I spent more time than usual visiting my aunts and uncles, friends and neighbors like Allie and Alfred Lang, and cousins, many of whom now lived in nearby towns. Some couldn't begin to imagine college in Mexico; most were polite, some saying, like my cousin Wilene who would have had trouble finding Mexico on a map, "Why, I think that's just nice."

One late September morning in 1954, I drove out the driveway of our farm in my 1950 four-door Ford with plastic seat covers. In the rearview mirror an image was burned into my brain: I saw my mother and father, tired and resigned, standing alongside the road as their last child drove off forever toward an incomprehensible and even suspect place. I'd left them alone in their old age. It wasn't "guilt" (another emotion not then in my vocabulary) that I felt, just a deep, unassuageable sadness. Writing these lines, I can see that I never got over it. I did, however, after Mexico, return to Goshen Township many times, even after the farm was sold and the buildings razed. I returned to bury my mother and father in their own land, to scatter the ashes of my beloved sister Irene.

21
Swept Away

The transformation of our family farm in Goshen Township and, on a larger screen, the sweeping changes in our lives in the years following the mid-1950s took place against the background of a much larger, global process. This included falling *real* grain and livestock prices and adverse terms of trade for agricultural products. In my family's part of Kansas, a series of underlying, worldwide "structural" changes, only dimly perceived in the fifties, turned out to be more influential in the fate of our farm than tornados or dust storms. What we thought would be beneficial for us, and the beginning of a new age of prosperity, led to the end of the century-long, 160-acre family farm and, with it, the end of a densely populated rural culture turning around family, school, church, and community: a culture that—if rustic and limited, and one that required a lot of very hard work—nevertheless provided the rewards of independence, self-respect, and a multitude of simple pleasures. I don't want to lament the disappearance of inefficient, smaller family farms that, given the values and methods then present, was perhaps inevitable, or to fall into a false sentimentality about rural life that only arose among city folk after family farms disappeared, but to remember that in my part of Kansas, the triumph of one way of life over another came at a cost.

———

Policymakers in Franklin Roosevelt's New Deal wrestled mightily with the effects of the Great Depression, beginning, in 1933, with a "planned scarcity" strategy that encouraged farmers to plant less, store harvested grain rather than sell, and required the killing of hogs (the notion that had so outraged my father) to drive up prices. This plan was abandoned in 1935 and replaced with a public works strategy, the

Works Progress Administration (WPA), which pumped $119 million into Kansas alone, designed to "return the unemployed to the work force."[1] This, alas, led to a second serious downturn in 1937; low prices for the things we produced and no relief from the Depression continued until the eve of World War II.

Then came the war-induced demand as a result of massive public spending after the Pearl Harbor attack. War industries manufactured 60,000 airplanes, 45,000 tanks, a great many ships of all kinds, together with the investment needed to support 16 million men and women in the armed forces and another 60 million in war-related jobs.[2] This created a powerful demand for commodities and a thriving economy. Prices for farm products rose 42 percent while our costs fell to 16 percent. The prices for all the farm products we sold—wheat, corn, livestock, eggs, and cream—remained high throughout the 1940s and into the early 50s. The war was good, if not for the soldiers that went off to foreign campaigns, at least for my family and, generally, for Kansas farmers.

My father bought a used Caterpillar tractor and began terracing our fields; at the same time, he acquired a Case hay baler and began doing custom work for neighbors. We also bought a better refrigerator, an electric sewing machine, a modern radio, a black-and-white TV, and a year-old Mercury. Apart from another severe drought in the early fifties in some parts of eastern Kansas, my parents and their neighbors in the early postwar years generally flourished.

Nevertheless, in the early fifties, following a trend already visible in the war years, young people, now in growing numbers, continued to leave the farm, and with fewer family field hands available, their parents, too, began to sell out. Perhaps most important in the exodus was a questioning, restless change in values and attitudes that became apparent in the postwar generation. Men and women who returned from military service or from work in defense plants or who had been able to travel to other states, taking advantage of easier access to planes and trains, came home changed while the world they had left behind had not. Having seen more of the world, including the great cities of Europe or those in the United States where they had gone on leave, or even experiencing a life-changing view from the rim of a foxhole, or having met other soldiers or sailors from different ways of life undergoing previously unheard-of experience . . . all this suddenly made everything at home look smaller. The barn cupola or grain elevator was no longer the tallest building we'd seen; there were dance halls and girls in the larger towns; army buddies told of living in states where you could actually order a highball or a whisky sour. I wrote in my diary on July 9, 1953, that "I walked back from Les Halles, I believe the prettiest time in Paris is walking across the Seine as daylight begins to break." A few former farm kids—not many in our neighborhood—took advantage of the G.I. Bill and entered college.

Enterprising young women also left. The first of our extended family that I remember making the transition to city folk were Kay and Ellen, two of Great-Uncle Gus's six daughters. They both went off to Santa Barbara, California; one married a chef, the other a dentist, and now and then they returned for short visits, coming back on the Santa Fe line looking very grand in high heels and elegant hats, telling of beaches, exotic food, dry martinis, porters, waiters, how one tipped, and other remarkable and unheard-of things.

——◆——

For those young people who might have been interested in staying on their families' farms when they returned from the war, they inevitably wondered whether the income from 160 acres would provide enough to marry and raise children. For others, who might want to buy a larger farm, the entry costs were high; now, by the 1960s, the old 160-acre farm would no longer do—and unlike in 1860, you couldn't push on west, stake out a homestead in the virgin prairie. In other words, there weren't many farms around to buy. Then too, having seen other worlds and other ways of making a living, it was impressed upon the generation returning from the war that farmwork was *hard work* involving long hours and unpredictable income. Here was the main question for a great many of the young men and women of my generation—although they wouldn't have expressed it in such fancy terms: *would returning to the farm provide an income commensurate with their newfound desires?* If not, why toil from dawn to dusk when you could make at least a decent living working nine to five in town?

In a short time, the answer was found. Uncle Walter and Aunt Helen's son found a job in the parts department of a pickup truck agency in Clay Center; a cousin, Harlan Riechers, wounded in Korea, got a job in the Post Office; Donnie Hofmann became a mechanic in Los Angeles and later in Arizona. Others went into construction, worked in filling stations, drove buses, sold cars, or tended bar at the aptly named Idle Hour pool hall. And so, like dozens of others in our neighborhood, we—my sisters and I—left the farm. My older sister, Lucille, got an office job in Wichita; the younger, fearless, and more ambitious Irene ultimately found a career in the American Foreign Service. And I, as we've seen, headed south for Mexico City.

The demise of the foundational, quarter-section family farm in the space of a single generation was not, of course, a simple affair or purely a matter of individual choice: much larger forces were working their way through the rustic world of Goshen Township. To paraphrase the classic explanation of a man much smarter than I, "people make their own history but not exactly as they please but under circumstances already present; they do not choose those circumstances." And the circumstances were rapidly changing.

There were many reasons for this. Through better plant selection, botanists, beginning in the 1930s in Mexico and India, developed a "dwarf" variety of wheat that by the early 1960s doubled global yields; hybrid corn produced similar results. Heedless of possible dangers, we poured on the herbicides, pesticides, and chemical fertilizers. In the 1950s and early 60s, my relatives and their neighbors enjoyed low prices for gasoline and the efficiency of new and larger tractors. The few remaining draft horses were turned into glue; the 60-horsepower, all-purpose tractor gave way to new 130-horsepower machines, and then to even more impressive and powerful 235-horsepower giants.

It's hard to exaggerate the importance of that single machine, the farm tractor, in the massive postwar increase in agricultural output. In 1920, for example, farmers employed 25 million horses and mules in agriculture in the United States, and 200,000 tractors; only three decades later, in 1955, there were 700,000 horses and mules and 4 million tractors.[3] Not only could one man seated in a comfortable tractor cab cultivate many times the number of acres possible with a team of horses, the land previously dedicated to pasture or grain for horses could now be devoted to cash crops.

Cousin Homer and his son Dudley were proud to show relatives who came to their house for Thanksgiving or Christmas the new machinery sheds, and they marveled over these gleaming monsters. They kicked the tires and climbed into the comfortable cabs, filled with admiration. The same increase in tractor size and price occurred in the development of self-propelled combine harvesters; four- and then six-row corn pickers became available as did far grander grain drills for planting wheat. This entire range of improved machinery permitted farmers to produce and harvest more of the new plants and feed more livestock for sale. Size not only mattered, it was essential given the need to plow and cultivate more land.

The new varieties of plants and greater efficiency in producing them led to higher yields not only in Kansas but also across much of the world as far as India or Argentina. This meant that in the late 1950s into the early 60s, the prices for what we produced stayed pretty much the same or at least didn't increase very much, but we could always produce more to make up the difference in lower price. As an example of this, wheat prices in the 1950s were about $1.90 a bushel and thirty years later, by the 1980s, were around $2.80, a striking decline in *real* (when adjusted for inflation) terms. This trend was also true of other things my parents sold: prices for cattle and hogs, chickens, and eggs all stayed relatively low.

At the same time, relative to the things *we sold*, the prices for things we had *to buy*—or thought we had to buy—went up. The new car my father bought in 1950 cost about 890 bushels of wheat; thirty years later it would have cost 3,000 or 4,000 bushels. A tractor in the 1950s cost around $3,000; soon, the new (and more powerful) tractors cost five times as much, one of the new, larger ones, over $50,000 by 1975, and many thousands more today. The term for this among economists is "adverse terms of trade."

For the farms in our neighborhood, the lower price we got for what we sold compared with the higher price for what we bought meant that a 160-acre farm, the size of the original homestead, no longer came close to supporting a family. To keep up, farmers had to produce more and this meant the acquisition of more land. Some came to operate not just 320 acres, but 640, then 960, and then much more. The smaller operators, the original "family farmers" of 80-, 160-, or 320-acre farms that began with the mid-nineteenth-century homesteads and lasted for a century, were fighting an outgoing tide: they fell by the wayside, the owners rented or sold their land, and moved to town.

These profound changes moving through Clay County were not lost on one Clara Blake, whose story appeared in *The Kansas Author's Club Yearbook* in 1961. Rather than a text on political economy, Mrs. Blake takes the New Testament as her point of departure. She pictures Jesus on a mountaintop in Nazareth; looking toward "the large and beautiful city of Jerusalem, teeming with commerce and wickedness, Jesus wept."

"Today," she wrote, "the remnant of our country's farmers stand with their backs to years of birthright and training looking down the road toward the cities. They have seen their neighbors going down this road, the cry of the auctioneer in their ears . . . their homes stand desolate . . . buses whisk the farmer's children to school; the country school houses, once so important, have passed from the scene."

"Today's farmer," she continued, "feels he has been hoisted on the petard of his own mechanical skill and technical know-how, producing too much food in a world where the majority are always hungry, ground between the upper and nether millstones of high costs and the increasingly lower price of his products."

The farmer turns to the agricultural agents and to his government officials. "Farmers must be liquidated," they tell him, "farms must be larger and become a corporate business, no longer a way of life. Truly today's farmers too, are facing the city . . . and many of them weep."[4]

Actually, Clara didn't have it quite right. "Family farms" continued to exist. In fact, individuals or families today own 98 percent of all farms in the United States. But the label "family farm" has acquired a new meaning. Farm size has dramatically increased so that today, only 7 percent of "family farms" in the United States produce 41 percent of all agricultural output. Only 2 percent of all farms under corporate control produce an additional 14 percent. Consequently, the agricultural landscape in Kansas (or in the United States) bears scant relation to the original, thickly settled farming communities of 160-acre family farms. The minimum requirement for a viable single-owner farm in the "corn belt" today, for example, is a property of 2,000 to 3,000 acres of row crops, some 500 to 600 hogs, together with additional acreage in other crops.

My own cousin provides a local example. Kyle Bauer—the grandson of Great-Uncle Gus—became successful in the 1980s. He, along with a few other younger people, took advantage of the new circumstances by learning to take advantage of credit markets and government policies. They learned how to get loans to buy more powerful machinery, how to turn the intricacies of the tax system to their favor; they planted improved seeds and employed new techniques and management, now often learned at agricultural colleges. Cousin Kyle, a graduate in agricultural economics from Kansas State University, with the help of only five equipment operators, was able to farm 4,000 acres (the equivalent of twenty-five 160-acre farms) of corn, wheat, and alfalfa; keep a keen eye on the credit and commodity markets; and, in addition, become the general manager of KFRM, an important regional radio station.

The deep change in rural life became clear from the 1960s on. The unfavorable terms of trade, the need to acquire additional land, and the consequent increase in farm size meant, of course, the precipitous decline of rural population, the sale of original homesteads, and the drying up of formerly flourishing rural towns. This is illustrated in what was our own, fairly typical part of northeast Kansas, the 36-square-mile Goshen Township. In 1880, the census counted 965 people, or 27 people per square mile. In the census of 2000, there were 92 people, perhaps 3 human beings per square mile.

The small town of Green had, in the 1940s, a thriving local commerce, including Walt Sweeney's grocery store and cold storage locker, an imposing grain elevator, three cafés, two churches, outdoor movies in the summertime, Fred Easterberg & Sons blacksmith shop, a (dimly lit) softball field, and many substantial houses. Today, the stores are boarded over, the gas station's empty, there's one tiny café, dust blows down the abandoned streets. In the 1920s, the census recorded nearly 1,000 souls; today the population is 147, including a single, presumably quite lonely, African American. The population of Clay Center, the county seat founded in 1860, dropped from around 8,000 in 1950 to about half of that—4,564—in 2000.

22
Epilogue

The last summer of my mother's life, in 1975, I returned to the farm from California to see her alive for the last time. She had suffered from dementia during the previous ten years. My father was living alone on the farm, the closest neighbor a mile and a half away. He had somehow personally taken care of her for the past ten years, but a few months before I returned, he had finally agreed to place her in a Lutheran hospice in the nearby town of Linn. My father and I drove there together, talking easily and affectionately, visiting on the way a cemetery where three of Anna's distant relatives are buried. At the hospice a stout nurse in a starched dress led us to Mother's room. She lay face to one side, on a narrow cot, her wasted body curled tightly in the fetal position, covered only by a single sheet.

My father stood against the wall. "Anna," he sternly called out: "Our son has come home." And then again, a bit louder, "Our son has come home." We stood silent for several minutes. There was no response, no movement, no more laughter, no more loving arms thrown wide in welcome as in those days when I appeared unannounced in the doorway of the farmhouse. No more flour-covered apron and that spontaneous tearful affection.

My father and I stood against the wall for several minutes. The nurse softly tapped and reentered the room, head bowed. "Will you be coming back soon for another visit?" she asked. "It does her so much good."

Five months later on a grey cold day in December 1975, I did come home again. Two men from the Neil Schwensen Funeral Home brought my mother out to the land she'd known and buried her in a proper casket in the Schaubel Cemetery, on a slight rise just north of the Alexander family homestead. Only a dozen people accompanied the black hearse out from Clay Center to stand in the cold wind at the gravesite. A few steps away stood the substantial granite tombs of her grandfather and father. The first homesteaded this farm in 1868; the second chose to leave the same farm on horseback when my mother was six months old, to die in the arms of a neighboring widow a mile down the road.

I went back alone that afternoon and stood looking across the fresh mound of my mother's grave to the curving fields of green winter wheat still close to the ground, over the dirty stubble of milo and prairie grass, and beyond to the now-crumbling Alexander house in the distance. This was where she was born and grew up, and standing by the tomb I wondered what her life had really been, what she was like as a pretty young girl, what she longed for or dreamed about at twenty.

When I was a kid she often talked about the "good old days," and I later wondered what those were for her. I believe she was often sad, perhaps because she felt unloved or unable to be close with my father. Or was I merely projecting my tired California clichés? Certainly, she would not have put it like that and I doubt that she had named for herself the source of her anguish; after all, one did not expect much affection.

Growing up, I remembered tears and cries of despair; I heard them often in the summers while sleeping out on the north porch while she and my father exchanged verbal blows in the kitchen. But I cannot know what she felt because such things were not talked about. When I worried out loud that she might do as she threatened and "run away," her only explanation was that she had been "blue" and that now "things were all right."

Left fatherless at the age of six months in 1896, the youngest in a family of eight (the oldest fifteen), and with her own mother an iron-willed widow, Anna Alexander grew up with the values of family and work and, in the end, wore herself out. My mother was tall—"as tall as Eleanor Roosevelt," she liked to say—merry, and irreverent. She was tender with "the little ones," her own and other children, helpful and loyal to her many women friends. She was a smart, observant, plain woman with simple tastes; as she liked to say about others, she herself was "as common as an old shoe." It may be excessive of me to apply the words George Eliot used to describe her humble Victorian heroine in *Middlemarch* to my Kansas mother: "The growing good of the world is partly dependent on unhistoric acts, and that things are not so ill for you and me as they might have been, is half owing to the number who lived faithfully a hidden life and rest in unvisited tombs."

———————

After my mother died, my father was no longer able to work the land or live alone. He reluctantly sold the property and moved—or, rather, was moved—against his desires to an old people's "home" in Clay Center. On the farm, our sturdy house and outbuildings fell into decay; scavengers came to pick through the fallen floor joists and rafters. A corporate group from Kansas City bought the land, introducing pheasants with the idea of creating a hunting preserve. That enterprise quickly failed and eventually other, more efficient, farmers appeared to buy the land.

My father's final descent followed the sale of his farm and possessions. Perhaps the effective end of his life—if not the actual death itself, can best be expressed in this letter I wrote to my sister Irene on November 15, 1979.

Very dear sister:

Yes, well, it's done. We—Rebecca and I—flew to Wichita on the Thursday before and drove up with Dad and Lucille the following day. We worked on arranging the stuff for sale but most had been done by cousins Homer and Wilene and above all, by Walter, Jr., and uncle Gerald. In any case the sale was Monday to a fairly large group of what's left of neighbors and the curious from towns some miles away. There were forty pies and sandwiches by the Ladies Aid, and poor Dad standing by while all of his closest friends (his tools) were sold off. The worst was his pick-up. When the auctioneer started on that, he said, "that's mine." I put my hand on his frail shoulder, remembering and missing the strong sturdy body I knew from when we were kids at home. He was helped, I think, by the fact that all around him were others—life-long friends—

who'd had their own sales, and were now in "rest homes" in Clay Center. They'd come out, curious to see the end of our farm.

Dad was very torn to sell off things in the house that closed off the illusion that he had a place to live and was still independent. Tuesday it rained us out—postponed to the twentieth of October—and I understand that things went well then. The whole thing must have brought around $30,000 or so.

On Monday, the Medical Lodge (an unfortunate choice of name) called aunt Helen to say they had "a vacancy;" i.e., a guest "had moved on." We talked to Dad about this and he finally agreed to "have a look at the place" on Wednesday, so I called and went over there and the lady, an upbeat, cheerful, superficial sort, of 35 or so, gave us a good welcome filled with institutional charm that Dad took to. Among other things she explained all the "activities" they had in the "home." Dad was making the point to her that he already had lots of things to do, like re-roof the house, mow weeds and so on. At one point she asked him if he "liked to paint?" He thought she was talking about barns, not watercolors, and acknowledged that his needed a new coat. But everyone is friendly and the place is clean and there are several people there who Dad knows. He was v. worried about the cost ($630 a month).

Anyway, anyway. We went back to aunt Helen's and the next day we presented Dad with the choice of going back to Wichita with Lucille or giving Medical Lodge a try. He sure as hell was never going back to Wichita but he had no intention of going to the old people's home either. But it did finally sink in that that was the decision he had to make. But he didn't like it. And it was not pretty or painless. We got in the car to go back to aunt Helen's and he kept saying, "This doesn't suit me at all." Poor, poor man. Our father. Stripped of his house and things on Monday and reduced to a cold blue room a few days later, I could hardly bear it.

A final touch: when Rebecca and I stepped through the door of Medical Lodge with Dad between us, it was Halloween eve. Incredibly, the lady administrators had not only got themselves up in blackface and ghostly garb but had put masks on the uncomprehending, hollow-eyed, poor old twisted creatures, a grotesque sight. Dad was v. confused; must have thought he'd entered a madhouse. Rebecca and I had a good cry on

the edge of his bed (he'd already gone over to visit his neighbor's room).
Memento Mori, little sister. When it comes to us we won't have thirty
friends and a dozen relatives in some God-forsaken old people's home to
comfort us. I'm less and less afraid of flying or of heart attacks.
Love and kisses. I'm glad you're not in Iran.
Yer brother

Four years later my father died. I flew from Santa Barbara, California, where I'd been attending a conference, to meet my wife and
daughter, Rebecca, in Kansas City, and we went together to Clay Center. The flag on the courthouse was at half-mast in honor of Dad's
many years as county supervisor. After I squeezed the rented car in
line behind the hearse in the procession, I looked in the rearview
mirror. A long line of cars slowly followed, stretching back at least a
half-mile as we made our way out the 15 miles to the Schaubel Cemetery and the Bauer family plot. After the burial, everyone went to
cousin Wilene and Homer's house for sandwiches, cookies, and iced
tea. Afterward, I returned to the cemetery and stood alone at the
freshly covered grave, Rebecca and my wife several steps back. Tears
and regret for all the things unsaid, the foolish disputes; loving memory of our endless work together in the fields, making fences, the
sawmill, wiring houses, baling hay. Remorse for the unexpressed love.

———✦———

Now old and bent myself, I returned with my daughter in the spring
of 2011 for the last time to what remained of the family farm we had
in Kansas. Flying into Kansas City, we stopped first in Clay Center to
see cousin Kyle Bauer and his family. Their large, attractive, two-
story, vaguely California Mission–style house with an enormous
kitchen, four large flat-screen TVs, a comfortable den, and a wrap-
around terrace sits on a knoll looking west across the fields to the
cottonwood-lined Republican River in the distance.

After lunch we turned north past the nearly abandoned town of
Green, driving the rented car slowly along the dirt roads, past the old
tumbled-down homesteads, noticing the fallen fences and dangling
shingles, the neglected, bare trees. As we turned down over the field

of what had been the driveway of our former farmstead, now plowed and sown to wheat, I could imagine the sound of the old John Deere plowing the field south of where our house once stood. I remembered the smell of our own waving green cornstalks in the rain, the storms blowing up out of the southwest, my sister running down the now-nonexistent driveway from the mailbox in September 1939, pigtails flying, shouting, "War! War!" I recalled the yellow headlights of Uncle Walter and Aunt Helen's Chevy—was it really a Chevy?—as they rattled down the driveway to visit—and then the cakes and rolls afterward—and a thousand things more: memories of long-forgotten things, of being young, full of youthful spirit and wonder, of being at home in the only place I've ever really felt at home.

Were a curious traveler to stray into the untraveled roads of these now-desolate regions where I grew up, he or she could obtain only a scant notion of the farms or people I've mentioned in these stories. The farms are nearly all gone; almost all our relatives—twenty-five aunts and uncles and endless cousins—are dead or have moved away; there are only dusty remnants of rural towns. The efficient new farmers, or farming companies, have cleared the land using bulldozers to push the abandoned houses and barns into piles of boards and stones. The trees along the creeks have been uprooted, the creekbeds themselves straightened out. Because there was only a tenth as many children left, the one-room rural schools were closed, the handful of remaining kids, looking forlorn in nearly empty buses, sent to town. Clarence Hofmann, the blacksmith, has long since closed his doors; the church is empty, the windows covered with plywood. A few kids driving by from one place to another stopped and broke the windows of Cass Kimbrough's store; rats invaded the shelves, and crows came to roost in the exposed rafters.

Here and there, every 4 or 5 miles or so, our traveler would see the occasional low, common, California suburban–style house dwarfed by machinery sheds alongside. Aunt Helen's place, the Langs', the home place, the Greys', the Rieks', and the Malls' are all gone. No more barn dances, no May-basketing, no chivarees, no hayracks hauled onto barns at Halloween, no community or church. White-tailed deer and wild turkeys have returned, beaver build their dams,

Alexander home place, 2011.

but there are no kids to run traplines at dawn before school in December or trip over frozen clods in the dark on the way to milk cows. There are no family gatherings at Thanksgiving and Christmas.

But there was something to be learned from this century of my family's life on a Kansas farm, and something to be loved.

A short walk from the Alexander place on a low rise across the road from a lonely patch of native prairie grass, the Schaubel Cemetery, enclosed by an iron fence, is still open for customers. The tombstones still stand over my mother and father, their decayed bodies lying faceup, side by side, deep in the earth. But no new mounds are visible; even death has ceased. The undertaker is out of work.

It was good to see that the graveyard was well kept.

Notes

CHAPTER 1. THE BEGINNING

1. Robert J. Hoard and William E. Banks, eds., *Kansas Archaeology* (Lawrence: University Press of Kansas, 2006).

2. This "long view" was inspired by Lautaro Núñez, *Porque Chile es Chile* (Santiago, Chile: Consejo Nacional de la Cultura y las Artes, 2010), a brilliant account of long-term national identity formation.

CHAPTER 2. FAMILY

1. Vachel Lindsay, "Bryan, Bryan, Bryan, Bryan," in *Selected Poems of Vachel Lindsay* (New York: Macmillan, 1963).

2. Clay County Court House, Clay Center, Kansas, *Register of Deeds*, vols. 40, 176, 302, and research in Steinheim an der Murr, August 1982.

CHAPTER 3. A FARM IN KANSAS

1. James Beck, "Homesteading in Union Township, Clay County, Kansas, 1863–1889," *Kansas History* 34, no. 3 (Autumn 2011): 186–205. I am grateful to Mr. Beck for discussion of this and other material, May 10, 2011, in Wakefield, Kansas.

CHAPTER 4. HOUSES

1. James Earl Fraser created his most popular work, the statue of *The Trail's End* in 1915. The image was reproduced in countless postcards and prints. Fraser studied at L'Ecole des Beaux Arts in Paris and also designed the Indian head ("buffalo") nickel.

CHAPTER 6. SMALL WORLD

1. Clay Center Museum, Clay Center, Kansas, "Green" Folder. The Clay Center Museum, located in the former hospital, has a large collection of newspapers, memorabilia, and troves of scattered, miscellaneous papers gathered into many large, imperfectly organized loose-leaf "folders." The archivist, Ms. Kathy Haney, performs a solitary and heroic task in making the material available to researchers.

2. "History of the Fact Community," unpublished, personal manuscript account in my possession, compiled by Cass Kimbrough, Walter Lloyd, Wandalea Sanneman, and Ralph Lang, 1954, pp. 1–13.

CHAPTER 9. FOOD AND DRINK

1. Mildred Armstrong Kalish, *Little Heathens: Hard Times and High Spirits on an Iowa Farm During the Depression* (New York: Bantam, 2007).

2. Kenneth L. Holmes, ed., *Covered Wagon Women: Diaries and Letters from the Western Trails, 1840–1849* (Lincoln: University of Nebraska Press, 1983), pp. 35–36.

3. Clay County Museum, "Green" Folder.

4. Lindsay T. Baker, "Blowin' in the Wind," *Kansas History* 19, no. 1 (Spring 1996): 6–21.

CHAPTER 13. MISBEHAVIOR

1. *Clay Center Times*, December 25, 1930, p. 1.

2. *Clay Center Times*, June 2, 1949, p. 4.

CHAPTER 14. CHURCH

1. For an excellent, comprehensive discussion, see Gary Entz, "Religion in Kansas: A Review Essay," *Kansas History* 28, no. 2 (Summer 2005): 120–145.

CHAPTER 15. SCHOOL

1. James R. Beck, *Toward a More Perfect Union: The Settlement of Union Township, Clay County, Kansas* (Clay Center, KS: Hidden Meadow Press, 2012).

CHAPTER 16. DEPRESSION AND DROUGHT

1. Clay Center Museum, "Green" Folder.

CHAPTER 17. HAVING COMPANY

1. Clay Center Museum, "Green" Folder.

2. Craig Miner, *The History of the Sunflower State, 1854–2000* (Lawrence: University Press of Kansas, 2002), pp. 25–26.

CHAPTER 18. WAR

1. *Clay Center Dispatch*, May 21, 1940, p. 1.

2. Patrick G. O'Brian, "Kansas at War," *Kansas History* 17, no. 1 (Spring 1994): 11.

3. Ibid., 9.

CHAPTER 19. TOWN AND COUNTRY

1. Clay Center Museum, "Clay Center" Folder.

2. Miner, *History of the Sunflower State*, p. 140.

3. Kansas State Historical Society, Library and Archive, Clay County, "Clippings," vol. 2. The clippings are arranged by date.

4. Susan M. Lang, "Number Please," *Kanhistique*, July 1994, p. 12.

5. For more on the history of courtship, see Beth L. Bailey, *From Front Porch to Back Seat: Courtship in Twentieth-Century America* (Baltimore: Johns Hopkins University Press), 1988.

CHAPTER 21. SWEPT AWAY

1. Peter Fearon, "Review Essay: Kansas History and the New Deal Era," *Kansas History* 30, no. 3 (Autumn 2007): 192–223.

2. O'Brian, *Kansas at War*, pp. 12–15.

3. Alan L. Olmstead and Paul W. Rhode, "Reshaping the Landscape: The Impact and Diffusion of the Tractor in American Agriculture, 1910–1960," *Journal of Economic History* 61, no. 3 (September 2001): 663–698.

4. Clay Center Museum, "Stories by Clara Blake," "Clay Center" Folder, 1–6.

Bibliography

Bailey, Beth L. *From Front Porch to Back Seat: Courtship in Twentieth-Century America.* Baltimore: Johns Hopkins University Press, 1988.

Baker, Lindsay T. "Blowin' in the Wind." *Kansas History* 19, no. 1 (Spring 1996): 6–21.

Beck, James. "Homesteading in Union Township, Clay County, Kansas, 1863–1889." *Kansas History* 34, no. 3 (Autumn 2011): 186–205.

———. *Toward a More Perfect Union: The Settlement of Union Township, Clay County, Kansas* (Clay Center, KS: Hidden Meadow Press, 2012).

Clay County Court House, Clay Center, Kansas. *Register of Deeds.*

Clay County Museum, Clay Center, Kansas. "Green" and "Clay Center" Folders, and other miscellaneous folders.

Cutler, William G. *History of the State of Kansas.* Chicago: A. T. Andreas, 1883.

Dick, Everett. *The Sod House Frontier: 1854–1890.* New York: Appleton, 1937.

Entz, Gary. "Review Essay: Religion in Kansas." *Kansas History* 28, no. 2 (Summer 2005): 120–145.

Fearon, Peter. "Review Essay: Kansas History and the New Deal Era." *Kansas History* 30, no. 3 (Autumn 2007): 192–223.

Hart, Douglas R. "The Agricultural and Rural History of Kansas." *Kansas History* 27, no. 3 (Autumn 2004): 194–217.

Herring, Joseph. *The Enduring Indians of Kansas: A Century and a Half of Acculturation.* Lawrence: University Press of Kansas, 1990.

Hoard, Robert J., and William E. Banks, eds. *Kansas Archaeology.* Lawrence: University Press of Kansas, 2006.

Holmes, Kenneth, ed. *Covered Wagon Women: Diaries and Letters from the Western Trails, 1840–1849.* Lincoln: University of Nebraska Press, 1983.

Ise, John. *Sod and Stubble: The Story of a Kansas Homestead.* Lincoln: University of Nebraska Press, 1972.

Kalish, Mildred Armstrong. *Little Heathens: Hard Times and High Spirits on an Iowa Farm During the Great Depression.* New York: Bantam, 2007.

Kansas State Historical Society, Library and Archive, Topeka. Clay County, "Clippings." 3 vols.

Lindsay, Vachel. "Bryan, Bryan, Bryan, Bryan." In *Selected Poems of Vachel Lindsay.* New York: Macmillan, 1963.